WRITING MONSTERS

How to Craft Believably Terrifying Creatures to Enhance Your Horror, Fantasy, and Science Fiction

PHILIP ATHANS
Foreword by
the H.P. Lovecraft Historical Society

WD
WRITER'S DIGEST
BOOKS

WritersDigest.com
Cincinnati, Ohio

For more resources for writers, visit www.writersdigest.com.

18 17   5 4

Distributed in Canada by Fraser Direct
100 Armstrong Avenue
Georgetown, Ontario, Canada L7G 5S4
Tel: (905) 877-4411

Distributed in the U.K. and Europe by F&W Media International
Brunel House, Newton Abbot, Devon, TQ12 4PU, England
Tel: (+44) 1626-323200, Fax: (+44) 1626-323319
E-mail: postmaster@davidandcharles.co.uk

Distributed in Australia by Capricorn Link
P.O. Box 704, Windsor, NSW 2756 Australia
Tel: (02) 4577-3555

ISBN-13: 978-1-59963-808-9

Edited by **James Duncan**
Designed by **Bethany Rainbolt**
Cover illustration by **William O'Connor**
Production coordinated by **Debbie Thomas**

DEDICATION

This book is for George, who hasn't had a book dedicated to him yet. Why not one about monsters?

ACKNOWLEDGMENTS

Let me first thank my intrepid interviewees, who lent their perspective, experience, and creativity to this book, making it infinitely better: Lynn Abbey, Scott Allie, Richard Baker, Brendan Deneen, Martin J. Dougherty, David Drake, Alan Dean Foster, Nina Hess, and Chelsea Quinn Yarbro.

And thanks to all the authors, filmmakers, and game designers whose work is quoted herein for giving the world some great monsters.

For everyone at the H.P. Lovecraft Historical Society—it might be possible to talk about monsters without leaning on the Great Lovecraft for examples of the best things that go bump in the night, but I wouldn't ever bother to try.

And thanks to Phil Sexton, Peter Archer, and everyone at Writer's Digest Books and F+W Media, but especially the endlessly patient and encouraging James Duncan. No one appreciates an editor more than another editor, and you, sir, are greatly appreciated!

"O, CREATOR! CAN MONSTERS EXIST IN THE SIGHT OF HIM WHO ALONE KNOWS HOW THEY WERE INVENTED, HOW THEY INVENTED THEM-SELVES, AND HOW THEY MIGHT NOT HAVE INVENTED THEMSELVES?"

—CHARLES BAUDELAIRE

TABLE OF CONTENTS

FOREWORD

BY THE H.P. LOVECRAFT HISTORICAL SOCIETY

It's a genuine pleasure to read Philip Athans's excellent book *Writing Monsters*. Monsters are just members of the family at the H.P. Lovecraft Historical Society, and sometimes we take them for granted. Around here we have Deep Ones singing solstice carols, and "shoggoth" is a job title. But Mr. Athans reminds us of the tremendous power of monsters, their limitless variety, their multivarious forms, their ability to terrify, to fascinate, to entertain, and to provoke reflection.

While Mr. Athans draws from an extremely impressive array of monstrous sources, we are, of course, particularly delighted to see the works of H.P. Lovecraft cited so frequently and so appropriately in this discussion. Lovecraft was indeed, as Athans states, a "master of the monster."

In Lovecraft's world, monsters are quite simply all around us all the time, and humans who read too much or look too hard learn this to their regret. He has monsters in every imaginable place: beneath the earth, under the sea, among the stars, on your doorstep, and writing insanely at the very center of the cosmos. There are alien races from other realms and times, god-like cosmic entities of unfathomable power, teratological hybrids borne of miscegenation, and unspeakable creatures stitched together by mad science, summoned by black magick, or revealed by fantastic technology. He even has monsters that make other monsters, such as the Elder Things and their uncontrollable creations, the shoggoths. Indeed, in Lovecraft's world all earthly life, including the human race itself, is the result—by joke or mistake—of the monster-making process.

There can be no doubt that Lovecraft identified with his monsters. In fact, he had virtually no interest at all in ordinary people. A difficult childhood, chronic ill health, and a precociously sensitive nature left him feeling alienated from himself and his fellow man. One of his early signature tales, "The Outsider," ends when the first-person narrator sees himself in a mirror for the first time and realizes that he himself is a horrifying monster. In "The Shadow Out of Time," the protagonist suffers a monstrous invasion of his consciousness by the Great Race of Yith—paralleling a multiyear nervous breakdown that Lovecraft suffered in his teenage years.

Lovecraft seemed to have the keenest appreciation for creatures that were not hemmed in by the constraints of time and space he felt in his own life. The Mi-Go traveled interstellar space and collected representative minds—the best and brightest—of the species they encountered. The Great Race could collectively change their physical forms and travel through time to capture information from every age. And even the bizarre Elder Things embodied traits Lovecraft valued most highly. "Radiates, vegetables, monstrosities, star spawn—whatever they had been, they were men!" Lovecraft's monsters were reflections of himself, strange in form, boundless in intellect, but able to exceed mere humanity through a mastery of the vastness of space and the ruthlessness of time.

But if Lovecraft sometimes thought of himself as a monster, the many friends and colleagues that he helped and encouraged surely saw him in a more favorable light. We sometimes forget that Lovecraft wrote more letters than pieces of fiction, many filled with thoughtful advice and support for other writers who were often younger and less experienced. Mr. Athans's book is in much the same spirit and will be of value to writers of all kinds, whether of prose fiction, scripted drama, games, or something else. May this thorough contemplation of monsters and its many well-chosen examples help to fire your imagination and in turn the imaginations of your audience.

Write your monsters well, but let them keep some secrets, too. Where some monsters like Godzilla and Dracula and zombies have taken center stage and permeated popular culture, Lovecraft's monsters have remained elusive, marginal, subliminal, and alien. Although we might occasionally wish that Lovecraft would receive the popular adulation we feel he deserves for his fundamental contributions to monsterdom, we cannot regret that even his most famous creations—Cthulhu, Yog Sothoth, the Colour Out of Space, and their fellows—have remained in the shadows at the edges of humanity's consciousness. That's where Lovecraft meant them to be, because that's where they're the most frightening and effective. Part of what makes any monster scary is that it is unknown and incomprehensible: It is weakened when it steps fully into the light.

Ludo Fore Putavimus,

Andrew Leman and Sean Branney
The H.P. Lovecraft Historical Society
www.cthulhulives.org

INTRODUCTION

REALISM VS. PLAUSIBILITY

"That was unrealistic!"

We've all heard this standard complaint from friends, critics, even ourselves after reading a particularly forgettable book, seeing a D-list monster movie, or watching a badly produced TV show.

It's a common criticism. But do we really expect realism from the fantasy, science fiction, or horror genres? Aren't these books, movies, and TV shows inherently unrealistic? Let's face it: As soon as a dragon swoops in, a starship engages its faster-than-light engines, or somebody turns into a werewolf, realism has gone right out the window.

Yet that single complaint persists. Those flying monkeys were unrealistic. That alien cyborg was unrealistic. Those vampires were unrealistic.

Admittedly this might be an exercise in semantics, but consider this: Do we find those things *unrealistic*, or do we find them *implausible*? A fine line separates the two, but for a genre author (in any media) it's an essential question.

Realistic implies that this thing, whatever it is, is true to its actual, definable, measurable, observable nature. A realistic description of a dog, for instance, would list only what we know about dogs, describing in detail a dog's behavior, appearance, and so on.

But it's impossible to "list only what we know" about a dragon, since there is nothing to know, factually, about a creature that doesn't exist. Instead, we have to try to make this imaginary beast seem real. Your readers know your description does not come via direct observation, like the description of a dog would, but you still need to make a case for that dragon within the context of your story's imagined world. You need your readers to accept what you give them, to have them say, "Okay, I'll buy that."

Readers and viewers of fantasy, science fiction, and horror want to leave the real world behind and explore a bit of the impossible. Very rarely is the fantastic nature of these genres hidden. The cover art, movie poster, or game box makes it plain that you are about to enter a strange fantasy world or a bizarre futurescape. Genre fans like "unrealistic." We understand that there's no such thing as a dragon, but we want authors to produce a plausible facsimile of one.

In all of the discussions of monsters that follow, this is the single crucial element that will drive us. Monsters can be, literally, anything. Your mythical beasts can be as big as you want them to be, your aliens as utterly bizarre as you can imagine. But no matter what, once you've set the rules for them and their worlds, it's up to you to abide by those rules. As long as you do, they'll come alive in your audience's minds, despite everybody knowing full well these beasties are entirely a product of your imagination.

Artist Francisco de Goya wrote, "Fantasy, abandoned by reason, produces impossible monsters; united with it, she is the mother of the arts and the origin of marvels." This is the genre author's primary responsibility. If you've asked readers to sign on to your fantasy or science fiction assumptions, you have the responsibility to make sure those settings—and all the scary and outré denizens of that setting—seem real.

Take this responsibility seriously.

HOW TO USE THIS BOOK

As the title would imply, this is a book about writing monsters. But before we can get too deep into *how* to write monsters, we should start with a shared understanding of exactly *what* a monster is (or as close to "exactly" as we can get), and why monsters exist at all.

Most fantasy and science fiction worldbuilding, including the creation of monsters, is a process of asking ourselves questions. In the first part of this book we'll ask questions like "What makes a monster scary?" and "Where do they come from?" This is the first part of monster creation. A monster that comes from the deepest depths of the ocean is going to look a lot different than a monster that comes from the deepest depths of space. They'll do different things, work in different ways. And asking the essential question "What's the difference between a monster and a villain?" is a great place to start exploring their inner workings, too.

Like every other element of a well-told story, monsters shouldn't just be dropped in for no particular reason. So in the second part of the book we'll move on to a deeper discussion of what monsters actually bring to our stories. What roles do they play? What do they represent to our characters and to our readers?

And then we'll get into the nuts and bolts of how to set rules for the monsters we create, how to bring monsters to life in vivid description that appeals to all five senses, and how to reveal monsters to our characters and our readers in a way that makes them scary, dangerous, and meaningful.

Scattered throughout are sidebars that'll give us a chance to look at some specific examples in five categories:

- **GREAT MONSTERS** looks at monsters from film and literature. How did they work? What did they represent? And why do they still haunt our nightmares?
- **ARCHETYPES** takes a closer look at common monsters that are up for grabs. How do we make sure that we've put a unique spin on creatures like dragons or vampires? What makes them "archetypes" in one book and clichés in another?
- **REAL MONSTERS** looks at our own world and finds the monsters hiding in plain sight all around us. What qualities do things like sharks and natural disasters share with fire-breathing dragons and acid-spitting aliens?
- **THE CRYPTIDS**, borrowed from the term from cryptozoologist John E. Wall, are a class of monsters that straddle the divide be-

tween real and imaginary. We're not 100 percent sure that they exist, but we're not certain they *don't* exist, either. I've lived in the Pacific Northwest since 1997 and haven't seen Bigfoot yet, but does that mean he doesn't exist?

• And finally, **MONSTROUS THINGS** reminds us that not every monster is made of flesh and blood. Ghost ships, cursed items, and nuclear weapons can be just as dangerous, and just as terrifying, as a giant radioactive dinosaur.

And we'll end by examining a classic story from H.P. Lovecraft that shows us how subtle a monster can be while still being scary—and this from an author not necessarily known for "subtle" monsters!

THE MONSTER CREATION FORM

Use this form to create your own monsters. By no means is this form an all-or-nothing tool; rather it's meant to help you organize your thoughts, answer some basic questions, and help you keep the *rules* of your monster clear and ready at hand.

Look for suggestions in each section on how to use the information to help you fill out this form. It might even be an interesting exercise to fill it out for one of your monsters before beginning the book, then complete a second version once you've read the book, and compare it to the original to see what you've picked up along the way.

But to start with, the first box asks, "What's it called?" You might know the answer right away, but you may actually want to leave it for the very end. And even then, some monsters, like the eponymous creature from the movie *Alien*, don't have names at all. Feel free to give your monster more of a shorthand description: *the monster from the sewers* or *the beast*. But sometimes, calling the thing by its name before revealing it in all its glory, like H.P. Lovecraft's Shub-Niggurath, the Black Goat of the Woods With a Thousand Young, can lay some terrifying groundwork early in a story.

You can download a larger version of this form at www.writersdigest. com/monster-creation-form.

THE MONSTER CREATION FORM

WHAT'S IT CALLED?

WHAT DOES IT EAT, AND HOW DOES IT EAT?

HOW DOES IT MOVE?

WHERE DOES IT COME FROM?

WHAT DOES IT LOOK LIKE?

    OVERALL FORM:

    HEAD:

    EYES:

    EARS:

    NOSE:

    MOUTH:

    LIMBS:

HOW BIG IS IT?

WHAT COVERS ITS BODY, AND WHAT COLOR IS IT?

HOW SMART IS IT?

WHAT MOTIVATES IT?

WHAT SCARES IT?

WHAT HURTS IT?

WHAT SENSES DOES IT POSSESS?

IN WHAT WAYS IS IT BETTER OR MORE POWERFUL THAN THE AVERAGE PERSON?

IN WHAT WAYS IS IT WEAKER THAN THE AVERAGE PERSON?

PART I

WHAT THEY ARE

When contemplating the nature of the monster, consider this: If you had never in your life heard the word *shark*, had never seen a photograph or video of a shark, had never learned about sharks in school or on Animal Planet, and one swam up to you, jaws agape, razor-sharp teeth crashing down on you, would you think it was a monster?

Author Alan Dean Foster defines a monster as "something alive and uniquely strange that we instinctively fear."

Sounds like a shark to me.

CHAPTER 1

WHAT IS A MONSTER?

A monster can be a lot of things, but ultimately it all comes down to one word: *scary.*

If you describe a creature that's no more threatening or frightening than the average bunny rabbit, it might be a weird sort of animal you've described, but it's not a monster. Does that mean every monster has to be a predatory animal, like the aforementioned shark or the H.R. Giger–designed nightmare beast of the movie *Alien*? This isn't an easy question to answer. Monsters come in all shapes and sizes, are created in all sorts of ways, and exhibit a huge range of behaviors.

Nina Hess is the author of the best-selling *A Practical Guide to Monsters*, a writing instructor of children's literature at the University of Washington, and an editor of fantasy fiction for young readers and adults. She defines a monster as "a creature of abnormal size or form with supernatural powers."

Based on her definition, a lion the size of a city bus (abnormal size) or a lion with wings (abnormal form) is a monster. A larger-than-normal lion, or one with wings, could also be dubbed "supernatural," but I don't think a monster necessarily requires a power or ability not found in the natural world. Would a giant lion that's otherwise "just" a lion still be considered a monster? I think so. After all, the giant ants in the classic 1950s B-movie *Them!* are "just" ants but are still one of cinema's great monsters.

Best-selling fantasy author Richard Baker got a bit more general in some cases, and a bit more specific in others, when he said a monster is "inhuman, it's animate, and it wants to destroy you. Many monsters are supernatural or [act] outside the norms of nature in some way, but that's not always necessary."

But does that eliminate the idea of a human "monster"? There are certainly plenty of those in fiction and film ... not to mention real life. But author Martin J. Dougherty believes that "a monster is something that is frightening because it is inhuman—it is hard to find human qualities (physical, social, or something else). Its behavior may be incomprehensible, or its appearance terrifying, or both." He does go on to say, however, that people—humans and aliens whose appearance is not disturbing—can also be monsters because of their behavior or values. "Likewise, a terrifying, strange creature might not be a monster after all once its behavior is understood."

This goes a long way to addressing our shark example. Once we know something about the great white shark, it stops being a monster in our eyes, even though it might still attack and eat us. Once we understand its place in the world, have some sense of its motives, it might still be really scary, but it's no longer technically a monster.

Horror author Chelsea Quinn Yarbro's definition is more general: "A monster is a distortion in appearance, behavior, and/or thought from what is seen as normal in the society in which the monster or monsters appear."

So does behavior alone dictate the line between human (or other sentient creature) and monster? For our purposes in this book, we'll focus less on humans with evil intent. Ultimately when we call someone like Charles Manson a "monster," what we really mean is that this man is acting like a monster and not that he actually belongs to some other species of creature.

These are all good definitions, and I've included them because the definition of a monster—what it is, what makes it a monster and not an animal or a person, and so on—will be at least a little different for everybody. What scares me might not scare you. So even though I'm about to define what a monster is, take this definition not as the final conclusion but as a starting point on which we can build.

In *The Guide to Writing Fantasy and Science Fiction*, I defined a monster as "any creature of a species that is neither a part of the civilization of sentient people or among the ranks of mundane flora and fauna." And I further simplified this by simply saying, "A monster is different and scary." It's something you wouldn't expect to meet on the street—including on the street of a fantasy world or the engineering decks of a future starship.

We'll talk a lot about what makes a monster "different" from villains, heroes, or humans in general, but let's start with the other word I have now mentioned few times. Let's find out what makes a monster *scary*.

CHAPTER 2

WHAT MAKES A MONSTER SCARY?

I'd like to meet the first person who ever ate a lobster.

Imagine being the first woman or man to pick up that horrible, red-brown spider-thing with terrifying claws and twitching antennae and saying, "Yum!" To me, a lobster is a giant bug with claws—I'd have run screaming from a lobster. But now we know what a lobster is and what it tastes like and that it isn't really dangerous. The only thing scary about it is the unknowable mystery of its "market price."

We'll want our monsters to maintain a greater degree of mystery, or at least begin with a greater degree of mystery than that.

Start by asking ...

WHAT ARE PEOPLE AFRAID OF?

I asked myself this question while working on a fantasy novel in which I envisioned a world overrun by demons. In an effort to build a sense of increasing danger in the book, each new sort of demon my characters meet is more dangerous, more powerful, and more frightening than the last. To do this, I decided to look at my readers' deepest fears and inject those fears into the demons. So off to the Internet I went in search of the top ten phobias. This is what I found:

1. Arachnophobia (fear of spiders)

2. Social Phobia (fear of a hostile audience)
3. Pteromerhanophobia (fear of flying)
4. Agoraphobia (fear of an inability to escape)
5. Claustrophobia (fear of enclosed spaces)
6. Acrophobia (fear of heights)
7. Emetophobia (fear of vomit or vomiting)
8. Carcinophobia (fear of cancer)
9. Astraphobia (fear of thunder and lightning)
10. Taphophobia (fear of being buried alive)

Phobias are irrational, pathological fears, though some of them are more rational than others. Most people are at least a little bit afraid of cancer, which is a highly prevalent illness that can strike anyone at any time. But there's a crucial difference between being nervous about a routine cancer screening and being literally paralyzed by fear of cancer when there's no rational reason for you to think you actually might have it. Phobias take common fears to the pathological level.

If these are the ten most common phobias (and I've found a few different lists, so your search may yield slightly different results), then there's a good chance that someone who is reading your book, seeing your movie, or playing your game will have one or more of them to some degree. And even if your readers don't completely collapse at the sight of a spider, they probably share at least a common uneasiness in the presence of one ... or worse, many spiders!

To create that sense of progression and escalation of danger, I simply reversed that top ten list so the final, scariest demon embodies the most prevalent phobia. That means the lowest-level demon comes up from underground and pulls you down and buries you alive, and the "boss" demon is a spider, or something that looks and/or behaves like a spider.

As it turns out, those are fairly easy fears to apply to a monster or demon, but what about pteromerhanophobia, the fear of flying? Richard Matheson made quite a splash in 1961 with the short story "Nightmare at 20,000 Feet," in which a poor soul suffering from pteromerhanophobia encounters the dreaded gremlin tearing pieces out of the wing of the plane he's flying in. This story became one of the most famous episodes of *The Twilight Zone*, a vehicle for a young William Shatner. So yes, a monster absolutely can prey on your audience's fear of flying. That particular phobia might be tough to handle in a medieval fantasy world with no airplanes. But what if the demons can fly? They might snatch up their victims and carry them off into the sky, release them into a free fall, catch them again, repeat the tortuous exercise, and toy with their fears. A reader who dreads air travel will squirm through that story.

But please don't think that triggering your audience's phobic responses is the only way to make your monsters terrifying. In a broader sense, monsters are scary because ...

THEY ARE UNPREDICTABLE

Can that lobster take your hand off with one of those claws? Turns out, no, but if it could and you weren't expecting it ... that would be pretty scary, right? In real life we know they can't hurt us, and that makes them predictable, and predictability is the enemy of horror. But add an unexpected element to a predictable situation and you enhance the potential for fear.

Humans tend to have a pretty good sense of what another human is going to do next. We can tell via body language, facial expressions, and tone of voice when someone is getting angry or upset. We sense when things might get out of control or violent. But monsters don't necessarily give out those human signals. This is a creature, after all, outside our normal experience. Who knows what it'll do next?

We'll discuss setting rules for your monsters and how important it is that you follow those rules, but keep in mind that while you know the rules that govern your monster, your characters don't. In fact, the less your characters know about what a monster can and can't do, the better. It's this unpredictability that will keep your readers on the edge of their seats, playing into the power of the imagination.

THEY HAVE A DISTURBING CAPACITY FOR VIOLENCE

Monsters don't just attack you; they attack you in particularly gruesome ways, as shown in this paragraph from the short story "The Little Green God of Agony" by horror master Stephen King.

> Melissa had seen where the thing came from and even in her panic was wise enough to cover her own mouth with both hands. The thing skittered up her neck, over her cheek, and squatted on her left eye. The wind screamed and Melissa screamed with it. It was the cry of a woman drowning in the kind of pain the charts in the hospitals can never describe. The charts go from one to ten; Melissa's agony was well over one hundred—that of someone being boiled alive. She staggered backwards, clawing at the thing on her eye. It was pulsing faster now, and Kat could hear a low, liquid sound as the thing resumed feeding. It was a *slushy* sound.[1]

Want to scare the crap out of someone? Go for the eyes.

It's up to you to set the degree of "goriness" your story will contain. Movies like *The Blair Witch Project* are terrifying without spilling a drop of blood, while some contemporary "torture porn" films, like the movie *Hostel*, are gross, even disturbing, but scary?

I tend to describe "gore" as unmotivated violence—a violent scene done badly, in which all the reader gets is a sense of the quantity of blood and guts without the emotional and psychological (read: character) connection of well-written violent action. For an example of well-written violence, I'll refer you to the scene in Haruki Murakami's brilliant novel *The Wind-Up Bird Chronicle,* in which a Japanese soldier is

---

1 From the anthology *The Best Horror of the Year, Volume Four,* edited by Ellen Datlow.

skinned alive. This terrifying act of violence is written with an impeccable hand for character, story, and psychology—but don't blame me if it scars you for life.

Take a second look at the example on the previous page from Stephen King. No blood. There is some yucky language in there ("It was a *slushy* sound.") but mostly we get Melissa's experience of this cringeworthy act of violence and her efforts, however vain, to make it stop.

Exploring truly disturbing events can be difficult for many authors to work through, in the horror genre in particular. But fantasy and science fiction—really any genre of fiction—can ask you to plumb your own psychological depths. So what scares *you*? A little creature that eats your eyes first? Is that disturbing enough for the psychological sweet spot you're trying to hit?

THEY EXHIBIT AN "OTHERNESS"

Monsters come from the Unknown (note the capital *U*), which is a place "out there," beyond our normal experience. The Unknown can be a physical place, or it can be more spiritual or supernatural. Again, lobsters aren't scary because we know where to fish for them, how they behave, and better yet, how they taste. But things that come from an alien terrain—literally an alien planet or some uncharted dimension— are terrifying until proven mundane.

In his short story "The Cold Step Beyond," author Ian R. MacLeod presents a world full of strange creatures hunted by a character who may well be a monster, too. This sense of his monsters' "otherness" is evident in a single line.

> The true aliens, the real horrors and monstrosities, lay not in the far-flung reaches of the galaxy, but sideways.[2]

---

2 From the anthology *The Year's Best Science Fiction: Twenty-Ninth Annual Collection*, edited by Gardner Dozois.

What an uneasy concept that is. We have at least a basic understanding of "the far-flung reaches of the galaxy," imagining that there are other planets out there with strange animals on them, but the idea of some other dimension, some place we can't even properly quantify, much less imagine, creates a greater distance between our irrational fear of monsters and our rational understanding of animals.

And in the story "The Other Gods," H.P. Lovecraft takes us to his Dreamlands—the ultimate Unknown locale in which sleep reveals an entirely separate reality, inhabited by things you wouldn't want to see in the waking world.

> But now they have betaken themselves to unknown Kadath in the cold waste where no man treads, and are grown stern, having no higher peak whereto to flee at the coming of men. They are grown stern, and where once they suffered men to displace them, they now forbid men to come; or coming, to depart. It is well for men that they know not of Kadath in the cold waste; else they would seek injudiciously to scale it.

And then there are the distant worlds of the endless universe, the epitome of the Unknown. "Much like a monster," Richard Baker says, an alien is, "inhuman, it's alive (or animate, anyway), and it wants to destroy you. In addition, it's definitely outside the norms of terrestrial nature or experience in some important way—it's not from around here, and the reader or viewer doesn't have anything in his frame of reference to understand the rules that govern the alien's behavior. He has to figure them out."

When it comes to aliens, veteran author Alan Dean Foster gets nightmares from the opposite of an invasion of some sort, from "the thought that Homo sapiens might be the only intelligent species in the galaxy."

To circle back to phobias for a moment, this idea that monsters come from "out there" plays directly into our underlying, or too-often overt, xenophobia—fear of foreigners. We don't know these people, and so we begin to apply what our imaginations come up with, which leads us to ...

OUR IMAGINATION MAKES THEM SCARIER

Albert Einstein once said, "Imagination is more important than knowledge." And the human imagination is pretty powerful. How many times have you imagined something will be absolutely terrifying—a roller coaster, a job interview, a scary movie—and when it's over you immediately say, "That wasn't so bad."

And another great quote: "The only thing we have to fear is fear itself." Franklin Roosevelt wasn't talking about Godzilla or Dracula, but he may as well have been. This plays back to the idea of unpredictability and "otherness." We have no idea what to expect from this thing and no way to determine its motives, so we start to fill in the blanks with conjecture, which tends to make something quite a bit more terrifying than it should be. Our imagination, and thus our fears, becomes the true monster in this case.

This application of our imagination can work in many ways. As stated above, we can fear something we don't know, but a lot of monster stories start with monsters that are scary and then turn out to be nice. The Beast from *Beauty and the Beast* is an example from classic fairy tales, and Frankenstein's monster is another, a creature who looks terrifying but is layered, emotional, and yearning for understanding ... and later, revenge.

In another way, creatures may seem harmless because they appeal to the softer, friendlier side of our imagination, but become monstrous when their true nature is revealed. *Star Trek*'s tribbles are an excellent example for this. When the crew of the *Enterprise* first encounters tribbles, their assumptions take over. They imagine the tribbles to be cute and harmless but have no specific information about their true nature. The tribbles slowly reveal themselves over the course of the story to be a sort of plague, like a swarm of locusts. Assumption and imagination can be very dangerous.

Play with the assumptions of your characters in this way, and you'll be playing with the assumptions of your readers right along with them.

We also have a tendency to assume that many of the sentient beings we encounter have a certain sense of right and wrong, or at the very least a sense of their role in relation to other beings around them and what they must do to not just survive but coexist and thrive, but monsters can be particularly scary when they seem to lack these assumed morals.

THEY ARE AMORAL

Human society, by definition, is a set of rules—or more accurately, a set of moral and ethical standards that then inform a code of laws. When a moral standard is violated there are consequences, which is why most of us know exactly what we can and can't do in public, what should be kept private, not done at all, and what will be offensive or disturbing to those around us. But what about a being outside of human society—some creature from another world—that doesn't have anything resembling a human conscience? A monster doesn't care how you feel, and it has no sense of the pain its actions cause others. It doesn't give a second thought to consequences or the rights, feelings, or treatment of its prey. Or, worse, it might have a truly immoral goal—not just the capacity for evil but a tendency to revel in the terrible, the violent, the grotesque.

There's something particularly unsettling about beings that do the "wrong" thing without any emotion or hesitation. In his novel *Excession*,[3] Iain M. Banks describes a particularly amoral monster in the form of an artificially intelligent spaceship:

> The Grey Area. The ship that did what the other ships both deplored and despised; actually looked into the minds of other people, using its Electro Magnetic Effectors—in a sense the very, very distant descendants of electronic countermeasures equipment from your average stage three civilisation, and the most sophisticated, powerful but also precisely controllable

---

3 Orbit 1996, ©1996 Iain M. Banks

weaponry the average Culture ship possessed—to burrow into the grisly cellular substrate of an animal consciousness and try to make sense of what it found there for its own—usually vengeful—purposes.

This thing simply doesn't care about its victims. How do you argue with something that doesn't even recognize you as anything but material? You can't, because ...

THEY ARE BEYOND OUR CONTROL

Humans generally like to be in charge. We spend a lot of time trying to control our weight, our relationships, our personal finances, our schedules, everything. We even try to control others by taking classes to learn how to train our dogs, motivate our employees, and so on. So what happens when a monster makes its way onto our starship and simply won't follow our rules? It eats what and when—and who—it wants to eat. It bleeds metal-dissolving acid all over the place without regard for the hard vacuum of space just a bulkhead away. You can't negotiate with a monster. You can't calmly tell a Denebian slime devil, "Okay, wait. I'm going to go to the store and buy you a bunch of steak—don't eat me in the meantime." That monster does what it does, and it neither seeks nor respects your opinion.

Simply put, monsters don't play by our rules—and that scares us.

THEY ARE TERRIFYING IN APPEARANCE

Here's another example from H.P. Lovecraft, from the classic short story "Pickman's Model."

> It was a colossal and nameless blasphemy with glaring red eyes, and it held in bony claws a thing that had been a man, gnawing at the head as a child nibbles at a stick of candy. Its position was a kind of crouch, and as one looked one felt that at any moment it might drop its present prey and seek a juicier morsel.

> But damn it all, it wasn't even the fiendish subject that made it
> such an immortal fountainhead of all panic—not that, nor the
> dog face with its pointed ears, bloodshot eyes, flat nose, and
> drooling lips. It wasn't the scaly claws nor the mould-caked
> body nor the half-hooved feet—none of these, though any one
> of them might well have driven an excitable man to madness.

Frightening, but here's an interesting take on description: Lovecraft goes to great length to describe a foul-looking creature here, but it is made more ominous by also describing what it's doing (gnawing on "... a thing that had been a man ...") and what it might do next ("... seek a juicier morsel."). And it's important to keep in mind that not all monsters have to appear classically "scary" in order to be so.

In *Miss Peregrine's Home for Peculiar Children*,[4] author Ransom Riggs describes a less traditional but no less unsettling creature.

> But these weren't the kind of monsters that had tentacles and
> rotting skin, the kind a seven-year-old might be able to wrap
> his mind around—they were monsters with human faces, in
> crisp uniforms, marching in lockstep, so banal you don't rec-
> ognize them for what they are until it's too late.

This monster has the ability to hit closer to home, describing the human potential to become inhuman through political, military, and/or social assimilation. Not as frightening as a "nameless blasphemy with glaring red eyes," but equally monstrous on the inside. As we progress through this book, we'll go deeper into what makes a monster scary by looking at symbols and descriptions, but for now, let's take a look at what I think is the principal reason monsters are so scary.

THEY TURN US INTO PREY

People are drawn to monsters because they flip the predator/prey rela-tionship on its head, turning us from the hunter into the hunted. This, more than any other quality, is what makes a monster truly scary.

---

4 Quirk Books 2011, ©2011 Ransom Riggs

Most people in our modern civilized world no longer think of themselves as "predators," per se, but we are still wired that way deep down inside. By nature, humans are omnivorous hunter/gatherers. And we're pack hunters. One guy with a pointed stick versus a woolly mammoth is going to go hungry. A dozen guys all working together with pointed sticks will feed the whole tribe.

One of the things that early humans sorted out, thanks to our complex, creative, problem-solving brains and our nimble-fingered hands, was how to kill things from a distance. That makes hunting safer. If you have to get close enough to a wild boar to stab it with a flint knife, the boar has an opportunity to fight back, but if you can shoot it with an arrow from several yards away, maybe even from the safety of a tree or some other high ground, you run the risk of missing but dramatically reduce the risk of being gored by your would-be dinner.

As the centuries stretched on, we became better hunters. Then we invented agriculture, domesticated the animals we thought tasted best, killed off competing predators in our chosen ranges, and eventually became fully removed from the predator/prey relationship. We are no longer concerned with being preyed on by other animals.

Then along comes a monster ...

What makes the alien in the movie *Alien* or the shark in *Jaws* so scary? Both are presented as *the* apex predator—"the perfect killing machine"—and it's loose on our starship or swimming through our beach party. It's *hunting* us, and our natural weaponry, which has made us a rather lazy apex predator over the years, is no match for its brute "animal" instincts and desires to kill and feed—and in some cases reproduce.

We humans still have those hunter instincts buried deep inside of us, but we don't have a natural enemy anymore. Monsters force us to find and use those instincts again, to varying degrees of success.

In *Alien*, we meet a cast of recognizable and relatable space truckers, and all of a sudden this *thing* is hunting them. They are totally unprepared to deal with the situation, and they're confronted with difficult questions: What is this creature? Where did it come from? We didn't know about this. No one told us this was going to be here. It just seems to want to eat us, one by one. It's treating us like prey!

They do eventually approach the alien as hunters would—tracking it down, trying to trap it when it's still small—but their efforts are complicated by the alien's inconvenient defense mechanism: acidic blood. The crew of the *Nostromo* can't shoot it. They can't stab it. They are, basically, defenseless in a face-to-face fight, which lands them a place at the bottom of the food chain.

What makes both the shark and the alien scary, even if we eventually win the battle, is that they attack when we're unprepared or unsuspecting. We either don't have our weapons handy (paddling around at the beach with our friends) or our weapons are rendered useless or dangerous (the acid blood eats through the hull of your starship and *everybody* dies).

And beyond negating our technology, monsters strive to isolate us. It's scary when we find ourselves separated from the rest of the "pack" like the arctic explorers in the movie *The Thing* (or the original John W. Campbell, Jr. short story "Who Goes There?") or the crew of the *Nostromo* in *Alien*. The creators of these monsters also create divides that separate the characters physically and emotionally. The Thing's ability to hide in plain sight breeds an environment of suspicion, where no one can tell who is good or bad.

THE MONSTER CREATION FORM: WHAT DOES IT EAT, AND HOW DOES IT EAT?

Does this monster flip the predator/prey relationship by eating *us*? That's definitely one way to make a monster scary, but what about the tooth faeries we'll talk about later in the book that eat your teeth first, then move on to the rest of you? *How* your monster eats you can make it even more terrifying than a great white shark. Does it use acidic venom to digest you from within (like a giant spider), or does it swallow you whole and digest you slowly (like a giant snake)? And even then, who says it has to eat people? The movie *Reign of Fire* imagines dragons that feed on ash—so first they have to burn down ... *everything*. There are monsters that feed on fear, on blood, on life force, on ... you tell me!

The most effective—and the scariest—monster stories always take away those things that humans rely on to tip that balance in our favor.

"A monster is something that turns life on its ear," says Scott Allie, editor-in-chief of Dark Horse Comics. "Whether its Gary Ridgway or Godzilla, it challenges how we look at the natural order, externally or internally."

This is the visceral thrill of the monster—the ultimate "What If?" What if you were being hunted down by something you didn't understand, something you couldn't shoot or bludgeon, that was stalking you in some remote location where you couldn't just call 911 or animal control? What if you were not just dropped out of your secure place at the top of the food chain but effectively removed from it—rendered defenseless, isolated, and obsolete?

The monster has turned the tables. Predator has become prey.

Scary stuff.

CHAPTER 3

TRANSFORMATION

At least as common as the reversal of the predator/prey relationship in monster mythology is the concept of physical and/or mental transformation.

Human beings are afraid of things we can't control, as I mentioned, and sometimes that includes ourselves. There's a deep-seated sense in the human psyche that recognizes the limits of our own self-control and that understands, although never quite accepts, the internal clash of the animalistic and the civilized. We tend to speak in what I like to call "transformative language" when this happens in real life: *He went wild. She lost it. They succumbed to a mob mentality.*

Time and again we're left to puzzle over the reasons behind crimes of violence, wondering what could make someone do such a thing, what has changed an otherwise normal person into someone—or some*thing*—who could commit, say, a horrific mass murder. We wonder how a whole society can transform into a genocidal mob, as it did in Germany under Hitler or Cambodia under Pol Pot.

That struggle for understanding might be at the very heart of our religious compulsion. We need something to help us control our own predatory instincts, and secular laws don't always seem to be enough. We want to stop that transformation before it starts, but failing that, we at least want someone or something outside our own natures to blame, like the Devil.

That being the case, it's easy to understand the success of monsters like the possessed little girl in *The Exorcist*. In the novel by William

Peter Blatty, as opposed to the movie adaptation, considerable doubt is left in the mind of the reader. Was this truly a case of demonic possession that overcame the laws of known reality? Or did this little girl, for lack of a better term, simply go nuts? Whatever the cause, *The Exorcist* is a particularly effective example of monstrous transformation. Some terrible evil force has infested this little girl, this perfect symbol of innocence, and a vile satanic creature takes her place.

We tend to be as protective of our physical safety as we are of our psychological health—if not more so. We know on a very fundamental level that if we lose a limb, recent advances in medical science aside, that limb is gone forever. If we lose an eye, we have only one left to risk. If taken to the extreme, physical transformation becomes not only harmful to our health, but a detriment to our standing in "normal" society. We inch closer toward that "otherness" we fear. For most humans, conformity, or at least the desire to be accepted and deemed worthy, is key to survival.

To emphasize this point, University of Notre Dame sociologist Elizabeth McClintock studied the effect of physical attractiveness in human mating patterns and found what everyone pretty much expected to be true: Attractive women tend to have fewer sexual partners, and those partners tend to be wealthier than average, while physically attractive men have many more sexual partners and don't give a hoot how rich the women are. McClintock's research hints that success equals attractiveness in men and that certain accepted physical traits equal attractiveness in women. And for what it's worth, what physical traits are accepted can change over time and from culture to culture.[1]

This sort of preprogrammed behavior is part of what makes transformation into a monster so scary. Deep down, there are many women, for better or worse, who feel that it's their looks that will help them get ahead in life, and there are many men who feel it's either their looks or their ability to achieve success that will—not to put too fine a point on

---

1 "Cupid's Arrow: Research Illuminates Laws of Attraction" (news.nd.edu/news/37481-cupids-arrow-research-illuminates-laws-of-attraction)

it—get them laid. But what happens when you lose these desired traits? What happens when you transform into a physically terrifying monster? What happens when you no longer fit the mold, when you lose your connection to the rest of the human race?

Not only are we frightened by the idea of being disfigured, losing a limb, or losing our physical or emotional selves, anything that has gone through a complete metamorphosis tends to creep us out. When that first Neanderthal watched a caterpillar go into a cocoon and come out a butterfly, surely he wondered, *How did it do that? I can't just go into a cocoon and turn into a completely different creature.* Even if you aren't afraid of butterflies, I bet you wouldn't enjoy watching a metamorphosis take place without some explanation of what was happening.

Throughout our lives, though, we do face some degree of physical transformation, beginning with our childhood as we grow from newborns into adults. Because this transformation from child to adult is natural, gradual, and expected, we accept it.

"I'm not sure if kids perceive transformation as terribly scary, actually," says children's book author Nina Hess. "I think they're aspiring to transform—they can't wait to be bigger and more powerful. So to them, the creatures that transform and become more powerful are probably more alluring rather than less."

However, as we begin to age, we transform again, and this time it's not so much fun. We often see cultures struggle with old age. Are elders treated with respect and sought after for their life experience, or are they shuffled offstage and seen as no longer useful? The answer is more often the unpleasant one, especially when terrifying diseases such as Alzheimer's—another transformation in which we lose ourselves—takes root. And on the physical side, the cosmetic surgery and cosmetics industries have certainly turned some tidy profits off our general fear of transforming into "old folks."

So when we put all of this together—the fear of becoming the "other," of transforming, of aging and losing our sense of self both physically and mentally—we find that a lot of our archetypical and famous monsters are transformed people: vampires, werewolves, mummies, zombies, pod-people, *The Thing*, *The Fly*, and so on.

Transformed monsters tap into some of the same fears as the superior predators we discussed in the previous chapter, but in this case, rather than dropping us off the top of the food chain or removing us completely, transformation into a monster drops us out of civilized society. Exile is something social animals fear as much as they fear a hungry predator.

THE MONSTER CREATION FORM: WHAT SENSES DOES IT POSSESS?

A transformed human may be stronger than any normal human, but what else might have changed? Does she have more sensitive hearing now that she's a vampire? Does he possess a more sensitive sense of smell in werewolf form? We'll talk about how monsters perceive the world around them, but this prompt on the form is really meant to ask, "What senses do we humans have that your monster lacks?"

Another form of transformation germane to our discussion is the transformation of ordinary animals into monstrous creatures. Examples of this include the giant ants of the classic 1950s monster movie *Them!* and the possessed family dog of Stephen King's *Cujo*. The two sit at opposite ends of the transformed-animal spectrum. On one end of the scale are the insects, spiders, snakes, and rats that we find scary and would rather not see grow to tremendous size. On the other end are the animals we happily surround ourselves with, like our pets, and those that quietly and naturally surround us, like birds (which certainly became monsters in Alfred Hitchcock's film *The Birds*).

Science fiction and fantasy author Robert Silverberg used this concept of animals transformed into monsters to great effect in his 1983 novel *Valentine Pontifex*.[2]

> He knelt beside the cage that held the rotund many-legged creature and made a deep rumbling sound at it. The manculain at once rumbled back and began menacingly to stir the long stiletto-like needles that sprouted all over its body, as though it intended to hurl them through the wire mesh at him. Nayila said, "It isn't content with being covered with spines. The spines are poisonous. One scratch with them and your arm puffs up for a week. I know. I don't know what would have happened if the spine got in any deeper, and I don't want to find out. Do you?"
>
> Yarmuz Khitain shivered. It sickened him to think of these horrendous creatures taking up residence in the Park of Fabulous Beasts, which had been founded long ago as a refuge for those animals, most of them gentle and inoffensive, that had been driven close to extinction by the spread of civilization on Majipoor. Of course the park had a good many predators in its collection, and Yarmuz Khitain had never felt like offering apologies for them: they were the work of the Divine, after all, and if they found it necessary to kill for their meals it was not out of any innate malevolence that they did so. But these—these—
>
> These animals are evil, he thought. They ought to be destroyed.
>
> The thought astounded him. Nothing like it had ever crossed his mind before. Animals evil? How could animals be evil? He could say, I think this animal is very ugly, or, I think this animal is very dangerous, but evil? No. No. Animals are not capable of being evil, not even these. The evil has to reside elsewhere: in their creators. No, not even in

---

2 HarperPrism. 1996 ©1983 Agberg, Ltd. Extended excerpt used by permission of the author.

them. They too have their reasons for setting these beasts loose upon the world, and the reason is not sheer malevolence for its own sake, unless I am greatly mistaken. Where then is the evil? The evil, Khitain told himself, is everywhere, a pervasive thing that slips and slides between the atoms of the air we breathe. It is a universal corruption in which we all participate. Except the animals.

Except the animals.

Valentine Pontifex describes monsters that are transformed animals and are clearly vicious beings, but it also shows some animals as victims, too. We feel protective of animals. Even predators can become lovable in our modern culture, as evidenced in the anthropomorphic lions, tigers, and bears that show up in movies, TV shows, and toys—the Teddy Bear and *Winnie the Pooh*, anyone? As much as we adore them, admire them, and want them around, when they turn on us, in real life or in fiction, it's horrifying, though we're well aware they're wild creatures to begin with. What the characters in these films and books are confronted with are not just dangerous animals, but also otherwise ordinary creatures transformed into something terrifying—and transformed specifically for the purpose of causing as much havoc as possible.

CHAPTER 4

WHERE DO THEY COME FROM?

Everything comes from somewhere, so where do monsters come from?

For what it's worth, it's not always necessary to be specific about where a particular monster comes from—you *can* leave this box on your Monster Creation Form blank—but there are certain "places" that are just as frightening as the things that call those places home.

Sometimes monsters are not so much denizens of a particular place as they are the embodiment or result of a set of conditions. Or, as fantasy author Lynn Abbey says, "I'm comfortable with an ancient notion of 'monster' as the unnatural thing that shows up after you've ignored or misread your omens. They're more like weapons (or MacGuffins) than characters: They're simply set in motion; they don't need (and shouldn't always have) backstories or motivations. And they serve as consequences—mistakes had to have been made, in innocence or by design—before they're unleashed."

But even then, unleashed from where?

What follows is an exhaustive list of every place a monster might ever come from, with the exception of all the other places I haven't thought of. That's a long and snarky way of saying that the origin of monsters is as limitless as your imagination. Still, here are a few of my favorites.

OUTER SPACE

The infinite universe is a fertile breeding ground for monsters even if you aren't working strictly in the science fiction genre. Science fiction, fantasy, and horror freely mingle in the cold, vast stretches of space, where unimagined environments might give birth to all manner of bizarre creatures and unspeakable evil can emerge from the void.

Horror master H.P. Lovecraft seems to have looked up into the night sky and felt more a creeping sense of terror and isolation than awe at the grandeur of the cosmos, as is evident in this passage from his short story "The Whisperer in Darkness."

> There seemed to be an awful, immemorial linkage in several definite stages betwixt man and nameless infinity. The blasphemies which appeared on earth, it was hinted, came from the dark planet Yuggoth, at the rim of the solar system; but this was itself merely the populous outpost of a frightful interstellar race whose ultimate source must lie far outside even the Einsteinian space-time continuum or greatest known cosmos.

In many (but not all) cases, alien creatures require a bit more homework than your average monster. Science fiction readers are a little more apt to ask, "Why?" in general. Why is this alien here? Why is it attacking the human colonists? Why does it have acid for blood? Why does it seem to be the only animal on its home planet? Thus science fiction tends to ask more from authors in terms of background research, but that doesn't mean aliens have to be less scary or wildly creative than fantasy's more magic-oriented monsters. "If it's 'an alien' as opposed to simply 'alien,' then it's something in which we can see ourselves and yet is fundamentally different: We can't grok an alien," says Lynn Abbey. "We might assume that an alien is intelligent and rational. We might even think we could understand or predict an alien ... but if it really is alien, we're going to be wrong. (Cookbook, anyone?)"

Another common thread between the monster of fantasy and horror and the alien of science fiction is the question of intelligence. Remember that famous line from the movie *Aliens*? "What do you mean *they* cut the power? How could they cut the power, man, they're animals!"

HELL

... or some other sort of Hell-like dimension. This is a place of pure evil and endless torment that has spat forth more monsters than any other locale in the history of the human race. Demons, possession stories, and the eternal struggle between Good and Evil, Heaven and Hell, has informed everything from the comic book *Hellblazer* to the novel *The Exorcist* to one of literature's great classics, Dante's *Inferno*. Here is an excerpt from *Inferno* describing one of Hell's more notorious beasts, Cerberus.

> Cerberus, monster cruel and uncouth,
> With his three gullets like a dog is barking
> Over the people that are there submerged.
>
> Red eyes he has, and unctuous beard and black,
> And belly large, and armed with claws his hands;
> He rends the spirits, flays, and quarters them.
>
> Howl the rain maketh them like unto dogs;
> One side they make a shelter for the other;
> Oft turn themselves the wretched reprobates.
>
> When Cerberus perceived us, the great worm!
> His mouths he opened, and displayed his tusks;
> Not a limb had he that was motionless.
>
> And my Conductor, with his spans extended,
> Took of the earth, and with his fists well filled,
> He threw it into those rapacious gullets.
>
> Such as that dog is, who by barking craves,
> And quiet grows soon as his food he gnaws,

For to devour it he but thinks and struggles,

The like became those muzzles filth-begrimed
Of Cerberus the demon, who so thunders
Over the souls that they would fain be deaf.

For the damned, Cerberus is an obstacle to be overcome; for the Devil, it's an agent, a guardian. What every denizen of Hell seems to have in common is a burning desire (pun intended, sorry) to get out of Hell, often with deadly consequences here on Earth. Some of the living have even tried to get into Hades. Either way, Cerberus stands guard.

When dragging a creature up from the Fiery Pits, consider what "Hell" really means to you, to your world, and to the people in it. Is it simply a place where the evil are punished and demons dwell, or does it represent something more complex? Does it sit in opposition to Heaven or some other dimension of good and redemption?

And is it enough to return a monster to Hell? How does this monster cross over, and even more important, why? And are there forces at work back in Hell trying to reclaim it or trying to send out even more monsters to torment the mortal world?

WE CREATE THEM

Since *Frankenstein*, authors have explored all sorts of scientific experiments gone crazy. And though we may feel we live in more enlightened times, if anything we're even closer to actually creating new life forms and technological monsters than they ever were in Mary Shelley's day. What would Mary Shelley think of the defibrillator, for instance, a device that brings a seemingly dead patient back to life through the use of electricity? It's hardly the same as her monster, stitched together from disinterred corpses, but give us some time. We're getting closer. Science is already creating bioluminescent goldfish and trees; we're cloning more and more kinds of animals for food and medicine; there's the infamous spider-goat hybrid! Not to mention engineered bio-weapons.

In his 2002 novel *Prey*,[1] Michael Crichton presented a contemporary Frankenstein in the form of nanotechnology—billions of microscopic robots—that escape from a high-tech research lab.

> It's midnight now. The house is dark. I am not sure how this will turn out. The kids are all desperately sick, throwing up. I can hear my son and daughter retching in separate bathrooms. I went in to check on them a few minutes ago, to see what was coming up. I'm worried about the baby, but I had to make her sick, too. It was her only hope.
>
> I think I'm okay, at least for the moment. But of course the odds aren't good: most of the people involved in this business are already dead. And there are so many things I can't know for sure.
>
> The facility is destroyed, but I don't know if we did it in time.

It's also possible to use scientific means to create new creatures as a way to peacefully solve some pressing difficulty. Anne McCaffrey, in her prologue to the omnibus edition of *The Dragonriders of Pern*,[2] gave us a unique origin story for her archetypical dragons.

> To control the incursions of the dreadful Threads—for the Pernese had cannibalized their transport ships early on and abandoned such technological sophistication as was irrelevant to this pastoral planet—the more resourceful men embarked on a long-term plan. The first phase involved breeding a highly specialized variety of a life form indigenous to their new world. Men and women with high empathy ratings and some innate telepathic ability were trained to use and preserve these unusual animals. These dragons—named for the mythical Terran beast they resembled—had two valuable characteristics: they could get from one place to another instantaneously and, after

---

1 HarperCollins 2002, ©2002 Michael Crichton
2 Del Rey 1988, ©1988 Anne McCaffrey

chewing a phosphine-bearing rock, they would emit a flaming gas. Because the dragons could fly, they were able to char Thread in midair, and then escape from its ravages.

These dragons were created to eradicate another monster, Thread, and became an integral part of Pernese society. It's fantasy and science combined. It's monster versus monster. It's problem solving using all of the above.

Ask yourself: What problems do my characters have that a monster could solve? When you build that monster, you can't have only that specific goal in mind. Even the genetic engineers that bred the dragons of Pern ended up with more than just flying creatures that burned Thread. These dragons have minds, and agendas, of their own. So if either your hero or your villain has created a monster for any reason, you must ask what the limits of his or her control over this beast are and what dangers await us when or if that control slips.

DISEASE

Zombies, Godzilla, some vampires, many werewolves, giant spiders, and all sorts of mutated beings are the result of a disease or radiation. Disease and its causes (viruses, bacteria, radiation, or genetic engineering) have only recently been understood in any accurate detail, resulting in a long history of strange assumptions, fanciful explanations, and barbaric treatments. People stricken with disfiguring diseases like leprosy or maladies with disturbing symptoms like epilepsy have unfairly been the sources of tales of monstrous transformations and demonic possession in the past.

But even now we're on the lookout for the next superbug, the next global pandemic, or the next bioterrorism attack. Diseases are scary, often because we cannot tell who's a carrier and who isn't until it's too late. In fact, one of the most frightening single chapters I've ever read is Richard Preston's terrifyingly detailed description of death from the Ebola virus in *The Hot Zone*. Late sixteenth-century physician Ambroise Pare reported case studies that seem, at the very least, to be exaggerations of actual instances of parasitic infestation, physically deformed newborns and fetuses, and so on. In his book *On Monsters and Marvels*,[3] he sounds less like a scientist and more like a B-movie screenwriter.

> Monsieur Duret assures me that he ejected through his rod, after a long illness, a live animal similar to a woodlouse which the Italians call Porceleri, which was red in color.
>
> Monsieur the Count Charles de Mansfeld, recently being sick at the hôtel de Guise with a high and constant fever, ejected through his rod a certain matter similar to an animal ...
>
> Many animal forms are likewise created in women's wombs, such as frogs, toads, snakes, lizards, and harpies.

This takes us back to the question of what makes a monster scary. Sometimes the part of our bodies a monster attacks makes the monster horrifying. (Remember King's eye-eating creature?) Here's another passage from just a bit later in *On Monsters and Marvels*.

> Monsieur Joubert (in his book *On Errors Made by the People*) writes of two Italian ladies: one was the wife of a second-hand dealer, the other a gentlewoman, each one of them delivered a monstrous birth within the same month; that of the clothes merchant's wife was small, resembling a tailless rat, the other of the gentlewoman's was fat, like a cat; they were black in color, and upon leaving their wombs these monsters climbed up to the space between the wall and the bed and attached themselves firmly to the bedpost.

---

3 From the translation by Janis Pallister. © 1982 The University of Chicago

Having been present at the births of both of my own children, I find this account highly unlikely, but it could make for one heck of an NC-17-rated monster movie.

Monsters created as the result of disease can inhabit any of the three genres: fantasy, science fiction, and horror. There may even be reason to view most of the current wave of zombie stories as science fiction. The thing that makes the dead walk in *The Walking Dead*, for instance, is clearly a disease, and one the CDC, before it's blown to kingdom come, has a chance to observe in action. Although the zombies appear to be creatures of fantasy/horror, their explanation is "scientific" enough.

In fact, this whole zombie apocalypse movement has drawn the attention of the contemporary equivalents of Ambroise Pare, like Jonathan D. Dinman, a professor in the department of cell biology and molecular genetics at the University of Maryland, who told the Internet science community redOrbit,[4] "I think that the Zombie Virus already exists (almost): Rabies. Infection is nearly 100 percent lethal, i.e. it turns you into the walking dead (for a while at least), and it causes you to change your behavior by reprogramming you to bite other people to spread the infection. Now if only it kept the corpse walking around."

If you decide to go this route, do at least a little research on how disease is spread. The most frightening diseases are airborne viruses—it's difficult if not impossible to stop them from spreading, and viruses in general can be extremely difficult to kill. On the flip side, things like sexually transmitted diseases or bacteria that require blood-to-blood transfer will spread a bit more slowly (at least until people start biting each other), and might be resistant to all the current antibiotics.

Does your disease mutate over time like the alien disease in Michael Crichton's *The Andromeda Strain*? Or is it scary enough in it's initial form? If it's caused by radiation, where does that radiation come from? Does it act on the victim's DNA to cause mutation, or does it simply kill

---

4 www.redorbit.com/news/science/1112964783/zombie-virus-could-be-reality-exclu sive-100213/#3vDa0T0G6r9XMzgW.99

you in some particularly frightening way? Diseases and radiation poisoning in monster stories have come from such wide-ranging sources as bioweapon labs, nuclear testing, the tail of a passing comet, a crashed satellite or spaceship, or the depths of the ocean … any of the dark corners of the Unknown.

DARK PLACES

We are afraid of the dark. We are not nocturnal animals. Our eyesight fails us at night. Look at the effort we've put into not being in the dark. Human history is a series of anti-darkness inventions from fire to candles to lanterns to gaslight to electricity. Thomas Edison is perhaps the most famous inventor of all time, primarily because he brought us out of the dark.

Because we don't see well in the dark and sight is our primary sense, we feel at a disadvantage when we can't see what's rustling around in the undergrowth at night. Is it a squirrel, or is it Shub-Niggurath, the Black Goat of the Woods with a Thousand Young?

William Hope Hodgson played on this fear of the dark in *The Night Lands*.

> Through four long years had I listened, since that awakening in the embrasure, when but a youth of seventeen; and now out of the world-darkness and all the eternal years of that lost life, which now I live in this Present Age of ours, was the whisper come; for I knew it upon that instant; and yet, because I was so taught to wisdom, I answered by no name; but sent the Master-Word through the night—sending it with my brain-elements, as I could, and as all may, much or little, as may be, if they be not clods. And, moreover, I knew that she who called quietly would have the power to hear without instruments, if indeed it were she; and if it were but one of the false callings of the Evil Forces, or more cunning monsters, or as was sometimes thought concerning these callings, the

> House of Silence, meddling with our souls, then would they
> have no power to say the Master-Word; for this had been
> proven through all the Everlasting.

What attracts your monster to the darkness? Is it simply a nocturnal hunter? Vampires, traditionally, are burned to death by the sun and are creatures entirely of the night. This is meant to set them apart in a negative way from the rest of humanity. The rest of us are awake and active and part of a community during the day, and we are apart from others, asleep, and vulnerable at night. So when a vampire (or any creature, really) is consigned to darkness, he's de facto shunned from the waking, human world, exiled not in place but in time. And again, as pack hunters, humans fear exile as much as we fear any competing predator—even predators that hunt at night.

"OUT THERE"

The concept of monsters that come from some unknown, unexplained part of our own world is as deeply ingrained in us as any other common fear we have. Just as we've removed ourselves from the predator/prey relationship—what Alfred Lord Tennyson called "Nature, red in tooth and claw"—we also tend to be territorial. Once agriculture took over our hunting/gathering lifestyles, we began to focus on defending our fields from scavengers and pests and defending our livestock from predators—things that come from places outside of where we live.

We also have a tendency toward the xenophobic. After all, other humans are the only animals we really have to be afraid of. I don't believe I'm going to be attacked by a bear in the parking lot of the grocery store, but my key fob has a panic button on it to help me ward off parking lot creeps. I lock my doors at night not to keep the Bandersnatch away but the all-too-human burglar. Add to this shifting cultural fears of those people "over there"—terrorists, illegal aliens, Somali pirates—and whether or not it's true, we sometimes feel surrounded by enemies.

All this combines into what ancient cartographers would define on maps as "Here Be Dragons." Beyond our borders ... could be anything, so let's assume it's not good.

King Kong comes from Skull Island—an island not on any map, surrounded by a perpetual fog bank. It's the unknown, uncharted, primordial wilderness. It's the jungle: the dark place beyond the tree line, where things are moving around. If you're out in the wilderness, past the edge of the map, not only might you be confronted by some creature you aren't prepared for, but when trouble starts, there's nowhere to run and no one around to protect you.

In his classic 1910 monster story, "The Wendigo," Algernon Blackwood cemented modern man's fear of the wild places.

> "The Wendigo," he added, "is said to burn his feet—owing to the friction, apparently caused by its tremendous velocity—till they drop off, and new ones form exactly like its own."
>
> Simpson listened in horrified amazement; but it was the pallor on Hank's face that fascinated him most. He would willingly have stopped his ears and closed his eyes, had he dared.
>
> "It don't always keep to the ground neither," came in Hank's slow, heavy drawl, "for it goes so high that he thinks the stars have set him all a-fire. An' it'll take great thumpin' jumps sometimes, an' run along the tops of the trees, carrying its partner with it, an' then droppin' him jest as a fish hawk'll drop a pickerel to kill it before eatin'. An' its food, of all the muck in the whole Bush is—moss!" And he laughed a short, unnatural laugh. "It's a moss-eater, is the Wendigo," he added, looking up excitedly into the faces of his companions. "Moss-eater," he repeated, with a string of the most outlandish oaths he could invent.
>
> But Simpson now understood the true purpose of all this talk. What these two men, each strong and "experienced" in his own way, dreaded more than anything else was—silence. They were talking against time. They were also talk-

ing against darkness, against the invasion of panic, against the admission reflection might bring that they were in an enemy's country—against anything, in fact, rather than allow their inmost thoughts to assume control. He himself, already initiated by the awful vigil with terror, was beyond both of them in this respect. He had reached the stage where he was immune. But these two, the scoffing, analytical doctor, and the honest, dogged backwoodsman, each sat trembling in the depths of his being.

Thus the hours passed; and thus, with lowered voices and a kind of taut inner resistance of spirit, this little group of humanity sat in the jaws of the wilderness and talked foolishly of the terrible and haunting legend. It was an unequal contest, all things considered, for the wilderness had already the advantage of first attack—and of a hostage. The fate of their comrade hung over them with a steadily increasing weight of oppression that finally became insupportable.

The monster from the deep wilderness "out there" is equally effective in fantasy—does your world have an "outback"? In science fiction, your characters might think *There's nothing alive on this planet ... we hope.* In horror, *We're camping out to make a documentary about the Blair Witch, what could go wrong?*

The unknown landscape and what resides there—very scary stuff.

UNDERGROUND

Humans aren't burrowing animals any more than we're nocturnal animals. Very few humans see the inside of the earth as welcoming. In fact, we tend to equate the ground under our feet with death, burial, and suffocation. Remember that list of common phobias? Being buried alive was a top ten fear. It's not merely coincidence that far-flung ancient cultures, from the Aztecs' Mictlan to the Finnish Tuonela to China's Diyu, imagine an Underworld beneath our feet inhabited by the spirits of the dead, as well as varied bestiaries of terrifying creatures. But in this case, we'll make the distinction between "underground" and "Hell."

Caves give us pause. They twist and turn into mazes from which we may never escape—and that makes them a potpourri of universal fears. What's living in there? It's dark. Because we're reluctant to explore down there—most of us are, anyway—our imaginations have taken over. Case in point, H.P. Lovecraft's "The Whisperer in Darkness."

> They've been inside the earth, too—there are openings which human beings know nothing of—some of them are in these very Vermont hills—and great worlds of unknown life down there; blue-litten K'n-yan, red-litten Yoth, and black, lightless N'kai. It's from N'kai that frightful Tsathoggua came—you know, the amorphous, toad-like god-creature mentioned in the Pnakotic Manuscripts and the Necronomicon and the Commoriom myth-cycle preserved by the Atlantean high-priest Klarkash-Ton.

When creating a monster from underground, you might think about researching cave-dwelling animals here in the real world. Does this creature even have eyes, living in a world of complete darkness? Or has it developed bioluminescence like many of the sea creatures from the deepest parts of the ocean, where no sunlight reaches? In the real world, there is very little life deep underground, so you don't expect to run into large predators, but then that's where your imagination comes in.

Your fantasy world may have something akin to the Underdark of the Forgotten Realms game setting and novel line, which features cities full of powerful races like the drow and the svirfneblin, raising the cattle-like rothé and fending off monsters too numerous to count.

UNDERWATER

The shark in *Jaws* resides beneath the waves, Godzilla came up out of the ocean, and so did H.P. Lovecraft's Cthulhu in "The Call of Cthulhu." Cthulhu is perhaps his greatest cosmic entity, a malevolent Elder One hibernating in an ancient city beneath the sea, waiting for the day when it shall wake and rise ...

I shall never sleep calmly again when I think of the horrors that lurk ceaselessly behind life in time and in space, and of those unhallowed blasphemies from elder stars which dream beneath the sea, known and favoured by a nightmare cult ready and eager to loose them on the world whenever another earthquake shall heave their monstrous stone city again to the sun and air.

Johansen's voyage had begun just as he told it to the vice-admiralty. The Emma, in ballast, had cleared Auckland on February 20th, and had felt the full force of that earthquake-born tempest which must have heaved up from the sea-bottom the horrors that filled men's dreams. Once more under control, the ship was making good progress when held up by the Alert on March 22nd, and I could feel the mate's regret as he wrote of her bombardment and sinking. Of the swarthy cult-fiends on the Alert he speaks with significant horror. There was some peculiarly abominable quality about them which made their destruction seem almost a duty, and Johansen shews ingenuous wonder at the charge of ruthlessness brought against his party during the proceedings of the court of inquiry.

Then, driven ahead by curiosity in their captured yacht under Johansen's command, the men sight a great stone pillar sticking out of the sea, and in S. Latitude 47°9', W. Longitude 123°43', come upon a coastline of mingled mud, ooze, and weedy Cyclopean masonry which can be nothing less than the tangible substance of earth's supreme terror—the nightmare corpse-city of R'lyeh, that was built in measureless aeons behind history by the vast, loathsome shapes that seeped down from the dark stars. There lay great Cthulhu and his hordes, hidden in green slimy vaults and sending out at last, after cycles incalculable, the thoughts that spread fear to the dreams of the sensitive and called imperiously to the faithful to come on a pilgrimage of liberation and restoration. All this Johansen did not suspect, but God knows he soon saw enough!

> I suppose that only a single mountain-top, the hideous
> monolith-crowned citadel whereon great Cthulhu was buried,
> actually emerged from the waters. When I think of the extent
> of all that may be brooding down there I almost wish to kill
> myself forthwith.

The depths of the ocean remain Earth's greatest unexplored frontier, full of bizarre creatures in an environment as hostile to human life as space. And because we know for sure that exceptionally scary, real-world predators reside there, like great white sharks and giant squids, when we look at the ocean, how can our imaginations not run wild with tales of sea monsters, from the siren to the kraken to the Loch Ness monster?

Science fiction authors can find the ocean just as fertile a monster hatchery as horror writers. James Cameron's movie *The Abyss* imagined aliens not from some distant planet but from the deepest ocean trench, and real-world scientists continue to investigate the possibility of life on Europa, a moon of Jupiter covered in ice that hides a liquid water ocean. What bizarre and terrifying beasts might live in that cold, dark environment, forever isolated from the sun and stars?

Since we don't yet know, it's up to you to create them.

THE MONSTER CREATION FORM: WHERE DOES IT COME FROM?

Well, what's it to be? Hell? The depths of the ocean? The limitless void of space? There is literally no limit to this. In the classic science fiction movie *Forbidden Planet* a starship crew is menaced by a monster from the id. This whole chapter will help you fill in this box!

CHAPTER 5

MONSTER OR VILLAIN?

In seminars and classes I teach, I like to put up a slide with a picture of Bela Lugosi as Dracula next to a picture of a zombie horde and ask: monster or villain?

Dracula is a vampire—not a normal thing in our world. By all rights that makes Dracula a monster. He is definitely a dangerous predator who views humans as a ready supply of food. A vampire has strange, supernatural powers that set it apart from the normal flora and fauna of the world. By every definition we've discussed, Dracula is a monster.

But isn't he also a villain?

Dracula was once human and was transformed into a monster, but unlike werewolves or other transformed humans (like zombies), Dracula retained his human intelligence. Dracula interacts with people, easily passing himself off as human. Dracula makes plans. Dracula falls in love. Dracula gets angry. And in more than one of his many interpretations, Dracula has deeply felt emotions—he even hopes for redemption.

Dracula moves the story forward with his actions, his ideas, his plans. That's what a villain does.

Zombies, on the other hand, aren't any smarter than the typical predatory animal, often much less so. A pack of wolves is considerably more cunning, creative, and adaptable than a horde of zombies. Zombies wander around until they sense the living, then mindlessly attack. In most zombie stories, they're flummoxed by things like ladders, low walls, and doors, which makes them relatively easy to avoid unless you're stupid or unlucky enough to let them overwhelm you with their numbers.

Thus zombies are monsters, not true villains, while vampires can be both.

What is the major distinction you can use when examining your monster? "Villains choose to do evil. Monsters are born or made that way," says best-selling author Richard Baker. "Plenty of creatures are both monsters and villains, of course. Dracula is a tragic figure, but (depending on the version of the story) he revels in his monstrousness."

Other authors have presented much more monstrous, less villainous vampires, like the feral creatures of the manga series Priest and its movie adaptation, but for the most part, like Dracula, vampires are intelligent, creative, emotional, independently motivated villains.

The creation of this sort of villain—or hero, as the case may be— should begin with the character first. If this sentient monster is going to be your story's villain, build the villain first. What does he/she/it want? What is the ultimate goal? What drives this character forward: why him, why here, why now?

I tend to define *story* as "characters in conflict." Every story is about people, even if those people aren't actually human. The rabbits in *Watership Down* are people. Spock and Worf from *Star Trek* are people.

Dracula is a person.

Once you have a handle of your villain's motivation, start building his or her monstrous side on that foundation. Ask yourself: How does this character's monstrous qualities help move my story forward? How does the monster's strengths complicate the hero's efforts, and how can the hero exploit the monster's weaknesses?

In his novel *Blackstaff*,[1] Steven E. Schend breathes "life" into a lich, which is a monster found in the Dungeons & Dragons game.

> The wizard wore olive-green robes trimmed with gold runes,
> a hood drawn up around his face, even though Damlath's face
> had previously appeared exposed. The wizard turned and spot-

---

1 *Blackstaff* by Steven E. Schend, ©2006 Wizards of the Coast, LLC

ted Raegar and the sharn's additional hands and began to laugh. The rogue gasped as he saw the wizard's hands were skeletal, as was most of his head. All that remained of his face was a shred of grayish-black skin across his forehead and down the right side of his face. Red energies glinted within dark eye sockets, suggesting eyes where no physical orbs remained. Around his torso and over his olive robes, the lich wore a harness made of black leather and a large round silver plate covered in runes.

Raegar had fought undead wizards and sorcerers before, and he knew that this lich had been impersonating Damlath, but for how long?

"Ah, Raegar. So now you know, little thief. Inconvenient. You've been a useful pawn even more unwitting than that dullard at the temple," the lich said, its jaws moving without lips and pantomiming magically produced speech.

Like vampires, liches are monsters with very specific strengths and weaknesses, falling into that category of "transformed humans." Steven Schend's lich, Frostrune, is as outré a monster and as cunning a villain as Bram Stoker's Dracula. What do they both share, other than this state of "undeath"? They both have names. They have histories. They have minds. They have *plans*.

THE MONSTER CREATION FORM: WHAT MOTIVATES IT?

This might be the simplest question to answer of all: BRAINS!

And that kind of thing works just fine for the mindless zombie horde—they just want to eat people. But if your monster is just a little bit smarter, there might be all sorts of interesting reasons for its motivations. If your monster has come from "somewhere else"—the depths of space or some other dimension—then *why* has it come here? Is it trying to escape Hades, or was it summoned here against its will and is just looking for a way home? Is it protecting something? Is it in thrall to some higher power? For this part of the form, start with as broad an umbrella as possible: It wants to escape back to Planet X. That single motivating force could fuel everything about the story from start to finish.

MONSTROUS CHARACTERS CAN BE HEROES, TOO

As hinted above, monstrous characters don't have to be villains. Mike Mignola's comic book creation Hellboy—and his monstrous companions from the Bureau of Paranormal Research and Defense—is a terrific example of a monstrous hero. He's scary to look at: a massive, red-skinned demon with huge horns he's cut off in a vain attempt to appear more "normal." At first glance he's terrifying—but then he speaks and seems no more a monster than any gruff New Yorker.

The idea of a monster that is revealed to be a hero is as common in science fiction (where monsters are often referred to as aliens) as it is in fantasy. As science fiction author and game designer Martin J. Dougherty puts it, "An alien is ... 'different.' That might mean completely incomprehensible and strange or just not quite right. 'Alien' does not necessarily mean 'bad,' but it does usually imply discomfort or suspicion. Once we are comfortable around the Green Blogwitz, he's no longer an alien, he's just a funny-looking guy from a distant place."

So as we continue to explore how to create effective monsters for fantasy, science fiction, and horror, the relative intelligence of those monsters will continue to be an important question. And, likewise, we can build monstrous heroes like Hellboy using the same sorts of elements that were combined to create Dracula or Frostrune.

GREAT MONSTERS: FRANKENSTEIN'S MONSTER

Author Mary Wollstonecraft Shelley created Frankenstein's monster for her novel *Frankenstein: or, The Modern Prometheus*. The book, first published in January of 1818, is arguably the world's first true science fiction novel.

The eponymous mad scientist brings the dead flesh of sewn-together cadavers to life through scientific means, inspired by the experiments of Italian scientist Luigi Galvani, who, in the late-eighteenth century, caused the disembodied legs of frogs to twitch when charged with electricity. There is no magic in *Frankenstein*, even if the exact methods Dr. Frankenstein employs are left to the imagination, and that's what makes the novel science fiction, at least as much as it is a horror story.

Author and game-designer Richard Baker likes Frankenstein's monster "because he forces us to examine the question of whether science allows us to do things that shouldn't be done, and what it means to have power without morality. Frankenstein's monster is not human from the moment of creation, and it acts in a villainous manner when it seeks to destroy everything its creator holds dear."

While not as sophisticated as Dracula, Frankenstein's monster develops his own individual thought processes and his own desires to become a combination of monster, villain, and tragic antihero.

Also implicit in *Frankenstein* is the idea of transformation. In the process of these dangerous experiments, Victor Frankenstein himself is transformed into a human "monster" who loses touch with the sort of ethical underpinnings that might have prevented him from completing his experiments in the first place. The monster itself is assembled from disparate parts of various dead men, and while his brain retains some of the memories of its previous life, it is transformed into something damaged by death, made into a violent brute confused and offended by its own existence.

Frankenstein's monster combines monster as metaphor, monster as a source of pity, and the visceral horror of an undead brute capable of blind violence. In turn, *Frankenstein* asks significant questions about the nature of life, the dangers of unchecked scientific and medical experimentation, and the responsibility of a creator for the misdeeds of his creation. Two hundred years after the book's publication, those questions are just as relevant, if not more so, than they were when Mary Shelley first proposed them to her libertine husband and friends on a dark and stormy night in Geneva in 1816.

ARCHETYPES: DRAGONS

The Greek word *drakón*, or "seeing one,"—the implication being that these huge serpents could see great distances—came into English as *dragon* as early as the thirteenth century. In the intervening seven or eight centuries, the word *dragon* has come to describe any sort of mythical or fantastical creature of serpentine or reptilian form.

In the Western tradition, dragons have become synonymous with greed, terror, and danger. But Asian dragons were spiritual beings of great wisdom and sophistication.

The image of the giant serpent is found throughout the world and across all the great cultures. It's entirely possible that these mythical beasts have their roots in reality. Surely fossil remains of dinosaurs were discovered, but not fully understood, millennia before William Buckland identified the megalosaurus in 1824. Chinese historian Chang Qu, for instance, reported on the discovery of dragon bones in the fourth century B.C. Other animals such as whales and crocodiles, and even extinct species of large flightless birds, may also have contributed to an evolving oral tradition that developed into our classic image of the dragon.

But whatever its origins, the dragon has become synonymous with the thing (or monster, if you will) to be overcome, and it's found in literature from William Shakespeare's *King Lear* ("Come not between the dragon and his wrath.") to J.R.R. Tolkien's *The Hobbit*.

Nina Hess, editor of the best-selling *A Practical Guide to Dragons*, likes that "dragons are fearsome and have unparalleled powers, but they can also be noble heroes. There's so much mythology to be mined with dragons, and they have instant wow factor."

Dragons are as much a fixture in fantasy as robots and starships are in science fiction, and like robots, no one has a trademark on these eternal creatures. By all means, populate your fantasy worlds with dragons, but heed the advice of author Patrick Rothfuss: "The problem with dragons is that everyone uses them. All the time. When that happens, they become commonplace. A lot of people think you can just throw them into a story and suddenly whatever you're writing is 28 percent cooler. But that doesn't work. All that does is make dragons into some boring cliché."

What makes anything cliché is a lack of imagination, care, and plausibility. Start with whatever mythical form of the dragon you like best, from the terrible, feral lizard of the European tradition to the spiritual transcendence of the East, but be careful to infuse your dragons with specific powers, physical qualities, behavior patterns, and cultural traits unique to your world and your story.

As David Whiteland reminds us in *Book of Pages*: "Imagine a land where people are afraid of dragons. It is a reasonable fear. Dragons possess a number of qualities that make being afraid of them a very commendable response. Things like their terrible size, or their ability to spout fire or crack boulders into splinters with their massive talons. In fact, the only terrifying quality that dragons do not possess is that of existence."

Dragons aren't real, so your dragon is no less a dragon than J.R.R. Tolkien's. Smaug is huge and red, and slumbers on a bed of treasure. Your dragon can be the size of a hummingbird, any color of the rainbow, and living in a library surrounded by dusty tomes of ancient wisdom.

Dragons belong to all of us. Make them your own.

REAL MONSTERS: SHARKS

Could the human imagination actually invent a beast as terrifying as the great white shark? If you never saw the television series Shark Week, what would you think of the creature described below? I used the exact same questions found in The Monster Creation Form in this book for the following description.

WHAT IS IT CALLED?
The great white shark

WHAT DOES IT EAT, AND HOW DOES IT EAT?
The great white shark will eat any living thing from fish to humans. Its voracious appetite is never sated.

HOW DOES IT MOVE?
Powerful and sleek, the great white shark can swim as fast as fifteen miles an hour, and it can breach, lifting its massive body completely into the air.

WHERE DOES IT COME FROM?
This prehistoric beast is a relic of the time of the dinosaurs, coming from the cold depths of the sea to prowl the food-rich shores near human coastal cities.

WHAT DOES IT LOOK LIKE?
OVERALL FORM: The massive great white shark resembles a torpedo, with a sharply pointed nose and sleek body that ends in a powerful, crescent-shaped vertical tail.
EYES: It has black, seemingly dead eyes that roll back in its head when it strikes.

MOUTH: Its massive jaws are lined with triangular, razor-sharp, serrated teeth arranged in rows, which are quickly replaced when they fall out. Its jaws can produce four thousand pounds per square inch of force.

LIMBS: The great white shark has a tall triangular dorsal fin that often cuts through the surface of the water, a warning of its approach. Its ventral fins resemble short wings.

HOW BIG IS IT?

The average great white shark is fifteen feet long, but they can grow as long as twenty feet and weigh upwards of five thousand pounds.

WHAT COVERS ITS BODY, AND WHAT COLOR IS IT?

The skin of a great white shark is as rough as sandpaper, though it appears smooth from a distance. A dull, almost metallic gray color allows it to blend in with the rocky floor of coastal waters. It gets its name from its brilliant white underbelly.

HOW SMART IS IT?

Thankfully, it isn't terribly intelligent, but despite its average-fish intelligence, it is a skilled and aggressive hunter.

WHAT MOTIVATES IT?

Great white sharks do one thing: feed.

WHAT SCARES IT?

Like most predatory animals, it avoids a fight when possible, fair or otherwise, and can be scared off by large numbers of defenders or by electrical sources that interfere with its senses and confuse it.

WHAT HURTS IT?

The great white shark can be hurt, but its skin is tough and difficult to penetrate with knives or harpoons. It can withstand considerable injury.

WHAT SENSES DOES IT POSSESS?

It possesses an electrical sense that humans do not, making it sensitive to electromagnetic fields generated by its struggling prey. Its exceptional sense of smell allows it to detect even small traces of blood as far away as a quarter of a mile.

IN WHAT WAY OR WAYS IS IT BETTER OR MORE POWERFUL THAN THE AVERAGE PERSON?

The average great white shark can easily outswim any human on Earth. Its jaws are capable of biting through even the heaviest human bone, and its teeth can shred flesh with ease. It can sense prey in the water in ways humans can't even imagine.

IN WHAT WAY OR WAYS IS IT WEAKER THAN THE AVERAGE PERSON?

The average person can easily outsmart a great white shark by hiding in anti-shark cages or using various chemical repellents, and advanced weapons can make short work of it.

THE CRYPTIDS: BIGFOOT

Although it's conceivable that there could be an elusive species of great ape out there that we haven't yet managed to wrangle into a zoo, despite reality TV shows like *Finding Bigfoot*, no one has actually managed to find one. But dozens of sightings of bigfoot creatures, or similar, are reported all over the world every year. In the United States, sightings are clustered in the Pacific Northwest (I always have an eye out for a bigfoot in my neighborhood—still no luck), Northern California, and rural areas of the East Coast, including the infamous Pine Barrens of New Jersey, home of the Jersey Devil.

Generally described as a shaggy-furred biped as tall as eight feet with ... well, big feet ... some witnesses report that the creature is hostile and threatening while others say it's shy and easily spooked. Native American folklore mentions the *sásq'ets* (later corrupted to *Sasquatch*) and often attributes various spiritual qualities to the creature, a phenomena much like the East-West disconnect with dragons.

The bigfoot creature has entered the realm of monster fantasy in many ways, from the hokey arch nemesis of *The Six Million Dollar Man* to the family-friendly houseguest of *Harry and the Hendersons*. He's also made the occasional monster movie appearance and is a reality TV favorite.

As with the other so-called cryptids—creatures on the cusp of myth and legend whose existence science has yet to confirm or deny—there are people who truly believe they are real, and given the fact that scientists discover new species of animals all the time, we should be willing to grant the possibility that a bigfoot-type creature is out there somewhere.

Still, they aren't "real" yet, so in the same way that Edgar Rice Burroughs was free to imagine a Mars that was very quickly proved to be fantasy, your sasquatch, yeti, or Bigfoot can be as wild a flight of fantasy as Burroughs's Barsoom. Is yours intelligent and spiritual or barbarous and ill-tempered? Do they have supernatural powers that allow them to remain hidden from sight unless surprised, or unless they want to reveal themselves? Are they apes, or are they Neanderthals or other early hominids, like the coelacanth, that survived long after science believed them to be extinct?

Author and editor Brendan Deneen has a soft spot for Bigfoot. "I love the idea of a creature living in the woods and avoiding humans," he says. "It's cool and tragic."

MONSTROUS THINGS: GHOST SHIPS

For as long as humans have "gone down to the sea in ships," reports of ghost ships have spread worldwide. In some cases, the term *ghost ship*, not to be taken literally, is applied to derelict vessels found adrift without any crew aboard. This has happened surprisingly often, even in recent years, and there are some mysteries that have yet to be solved. The most famous is probably the *Mary Celeste*, found adrift in 1872 between Portugal and the Azores. To this day, no one knows what happened to *Mary Celeste*'s missing crew, but the strange ghost ship has inspired some tall tales that were occasionally reported as fact, with theories ranging from pirates to sea monsters.

But there are also more literal "ghost ships," which, like the cryptids, eyewitnesses have reported as fact, despite their obviously supernatural nature. The *Flying Dutchman* is the product of the oral tradition of late eighteenth-century sailors. This tale of a captain doomed to pilot his crewless vessel and wander the seas for all eternity is a sailor's version of a campfire ghost story.

Ghost ships have sailed their way through many horror stories, including Captain Frederick Marryat's *The Phantom Ship*, a tale of the *Flying Dutchman* originally published in serial form in *The New Monthly Magazine* from March 1838 through August of 1839. The 2002 Warner Brothers feature *Ghost Ship*, starring Gabriel Byrne and Julianna Margulies, put a modern but very creepy twist on the ghost ship myth.

David Drake, author of *Hammer's Slammers* and other books, is fond of them. "Ghost ships or derelicts with something still aboard are good for only one note, but it can be very effective. The ill-fated ship in *Dracula*, the *Demeter*, is one example, but

I remember a story from the Not at Night series (some time in the 1920s) in which a German cruiser that disappeared in the Far East during WWI is found drifting—and filled with ticks desperate for a new infusion of blood. And "Three Skeleton Key" (by George G. Toudouze), in which the ship is filled with thousands of starving rats!"

Ghost ships don't have to be "one note," though—there are many types of "ship," including spaceships, and just as many meanings of "ghost."

And consider other ghostly contrivances: the strange driverless coach in *Dracula*; the phantom funeral train that is said to run from Washington, DC to Springfield, Illinois on the anniversary of the death of Abraham Lincoln; and then there's the demonic car of Stephen King's *Christine*.

When creating your own, think about ghost ships (and other vehicles) the same way you would a haunted house or castle. What has cursed that thing, that place? The ship (or train or car or starship) can be a monster itself, imbued with a demonic life of its own. Feel free to explore the existing lore of ghost ships and derelicts. What really happened to the crew of the sailing barge *Zebrina* in 1917, for instance? Google it, and let your imagination roam free from there.

PART II

WHY THEY'RE HERE

Everything that happens in a story must happen for a reason. And since neither science fiction, fantasy, or even horror actually requires the presence of a monster, monsters shouldn't show up in your book or screenplay "just because." In this section we'll discuss what monsters are for, what they represent, and how they interact with your characters and story.

"Above all else," fantasy author Lynn Abbey says, "know your monster and why it's in your story.

And why monsters at all? What is it about things that go bump in the night that we find so attractive that they've infiltrated every culture on Earth, every mythology, every art form?

Author Nina Hess admits she's no psychologist, "but I do think monsters embody many universal fears and desires—and the lore of monsters taps into the need to address those universal emotions."

CHAPTER 6

HOW "MONSTER-RICH" IS YOUR WORLD?

It's your world, we're just visiting.

This is especially true of science fiction, fantasy, and horror, although horror, of those three genres, tends to have the strongest connection to the real world. Horror stories—particularly monster stories—depend most on what we discussed earlier in terms of turning that predator/prey relationship around on us. Stories from *Beowulf* to *The Cabin in the Woods* explore the reaction of various groups of people to the sudden appearance of a supernatural creature in an otherwise commonplace setting. Fantasy tends to demand the most worldbuilding, as we saw in the fully imagined world of J.R.R. Tolkien's Middle-earth. Science fiction often presents a far-off future so remote from our day-to-day experience that it may as well be fantasy, like Frank Herbert's richly realized world of the 11,000th century in *Dune*. But even if you begin in the real world—either past, present, or future—once a monster shows up, magic is revealed, or some advanced technology is introduced, it becomes your world, not ours.

"In the classic monster story, the monster is essentially singular and unnatural in its milieu—whether that milieu is New York City, Barsoom, or Middle-earth," says Lynn Abbey. "Setting the story in the real world can free the writer from the need to explain not only what the monster is, but how the plumbing works. Setting it in an imagined world, though, frees the writer to tweak the danger variables ... and opens the door for some very odd odd-men." Abbey goes on to say that aspiring writers should trust their instincts. "If the story in their mind's eye is a monster on a spaceship, then that's the story they should write, but if the writing bogs down, then it can't hurt to do a thought experiment: Place the monster someplace else, or use the spaceship without the monster."

With that permission to decide for yourself, the first fundamental decision every author needs to make in terms of how monsters fit into your overall worldbuilding efforts is just how monster-rich your world is.

In general, you have three options. All three require work and imagination, but in different doses and to different ends.

REAL WORLD + ONE MONSTER

Just one monster tends to be the realm of the horror story, though not exclusively. There are plenty of fantasies, from *Conan* to *Game of Thrones,* in which monsters, in the classical sense, are a bit thin on the ground. The stories focus more on humans than any monsters or strange creatures. And science fiction quite often excludes them entirely. Likewise, in many horror stories, the "monster" is all too human, more in the line of a human villain.

But introducing a single, previously unknown creature to an otherwise predictable time and place can be, and quite often has been, extremely effective. Rather than being surrounded by many creatures, there's just the one, and if you can't see it ... it could be anywhere, heightening the fear, suspicion, and anxiety in your characters. And this conflict against one nemesis can put us face to face with many of our greatest fears. Consider the monstrous shark in *Jaws* or the mysterious shapeshifting alien in *The Thing.* Both of those monsters, on the purely primal level, stalk and prey on humans and upset that predator/prey balance, but beyond that they work on different sets of fears. The shark in *Jaws* played on our age-old fears of what lies beneath the surface of the vast oceans of Earth, which are unknown and uncharted territory for most of us. You can bet that far fewer people took to the waters the summer *Jaws* hit theaters. And the unnamed alien in *The Thing* represents the fear of a loss of individuality, and all that's scary about being absorbed, body and soul, into some truly alien thing. The single-monster story drills the focus down to a single conflict, but that single conflict (us vs. the monster) can work on multiple levels, giving us more than one reason to fear this thing that suddenly swam up, thawed out, landed, or otherwise inserted itself into our happy home.

When your entire story depends on a single monster, that monster had better be really effective and well thought out. Write a detailed character sketch for your monster, and immerse yourself in every bit of its existence, even if certain elements of its backstory, creation, strengths and weaknesses, and so on never make it into the finished product.

REAL WORLD + MANY MONSTERS

It's safe to say that the majority of fantasy falls into this category. Many a medieval fantasy novel finds characters riding horses, raising pigs, encountering packs of wolves, and so on—and then at some point the dragon flies, the orcs attack, and eventually the slithering *thing* emerges from the Dark Dimension.

There are some significant questions you have to ask yourself if you intend to go down the path toward a world full of monsters. The first goes back to our discussion of what makes a monster a monster in the first place. You may have many monsters in your world, but are they all going to be dangerous, deadly, or even "villainous"? If your fantasy world includes dogs, but some people also have unusual creatures called grothars as pets, then the grothar isn't a "monster" per se, but a weird domesticated animal similar to a dog. If you're presenting a world that includes recognizable animals like dogs and new animals of your own creation, keep a close eye on that definition of a monster: "any creature of a species that is neither a part of the civilization of sentient people or among the ranks of mundane flora and fauna." So the dog and the grothar are both among the ranks of mundane flora and fauna in your created world, even if the grothar isn't part of our real world. So in this case, your characters wouldn't treat a grothar like a monster.

These types of fantasy worlds aren't so much rich in monsters as they are rich in weird animals. In order to be effective, your true monsters in this scenario must be surprising to the characters who are used to the other odd creatures that inhabit your imagined world.

Alternately you can create a monster-rich world without any friendly or neutral creatures. Perhaps your world is essentially the same as medieval Europe, but then the portal to the Dark Dimension is opened and all manner of monsters enter. These could also be animalistic creatures, but it's not likely they have a peaceful intent. This can even work as a way to introduce a plethora of different monsters into the here and now, as it did in Stephen King's *The Mist*.

Fantasy readers tend to be a lot more forgiving of monster-rich ecosystems than science fiction readers are, and the latter are going to demand at least a general explanation as to how all of these monsters and aliens evolved, where they came from, and how it is that populations of monsters can exist side by side not just with humans and other sentient species but with other animals.

Keep in mind the ecological or energy pyramid, which describes living ecosystems as a pyramid, with smaller animals that require less energy at the bottom and very large predators at the very top. The pyramid illustrates that an ecosystem can support huge numbers of grazing herbivores, like gazelles, for instance, but far fewer large predators like the lions that hunt them. And if you're imagining a reality-based world that includes both rabbits and dragons, we understand where the rabbits fit in, but you'll need to explain how the dragons survive. How much and how often do they need to eat? And so on.

So where does your monster sit on this pyramid? If, as in *The Mist*, these things are aliens brought in from some other place, time, or dimension, then all bets are off. You're free to toss that energy pyramid right out the window. What if only the predators were brought through the portal? Or these monsters are coming from a world with scarce plant life so almost every complex life-form is a carnivore? Consider all ecological and environmental questions when writing your monster to avoid any unrealistic plot holes.

NO REAL-WORLD ANIMALS AT ALL

Imagine an entirely unique world in which no real-world animals are found at all. Science fiction authors will often find themselves in this territory by default. Why would there be raccoons on a planet two thousand light-years away? If your characters are the first to land on a distant planet, anything alive there must be one of your own unique creations.

In worlds like this, new creatures are created to fill certain niches that real-world animals would otherwise fill. In a world with no horses, there might be some other creature that people use to ride on or to pull carts. And if there are no chickens to raise or deer to hunt, what do the omnivores eat?

This is a real worldbuilding challenge. No one is riding around on a horse; no one has a dog; there's no crow flying overhead; there are no chickens, no pigs, no house flies—you have to create *everything*. So even as you're thinking about giant snake mounts or multitentacled guard beasts, science fiction author David Drake cautions you to "remember the little things. You don't have birds, but you can get a really disconcerting effect by having frogs flapping their huge webbed feet to fly from tree to tree."

Legendary science fiction and fantasy master Edgar Rice Burroughs took on this challenge in his stories of John Carter that began in *A Princess of Mars*. He created the calot, or the Martian equivalent of a dog. Here's his description of John Carter's calot, named Woola.

> Imagine, if you can, a huge grizzly with ten legs armed with mighty talons and an enormous froglike mouth splitting his head from ear to ear, exposing three rows of long, white tusks. Then endow this creature of your imagination with the agility and ferocity of a half-starved Bengal tiger and the strength of a span of bulls, and you will have some faint conception of Woola in action.
>
> Before I could call him off he had crushed Lakor into a jelly with a single blow of one mighty paw and had literally torn the other thern to ribbons; yet when I spoke to him sharply he cowed sheepishly as though he had done a thing to deserve censure and chastisement.

Though Burroughs's Martian calot is scarier than the average dog, the calot is a part of the mundane flora and fauna of Barsoom. It's a "monster" when John Carter first encounters it and has no idea what it is, but it becomes a "pet" when Carter gets to know this strange alien world—and Woola—a little better.

David Drake provides some advice for balancing your monster-rich world in a way that makes the existence of the human population plausible: "Ecosystems in which everything is a predator determined to destroy the hero are silly, though both *Tarzan* and *Cooperate—Or Else!* were very effective when I was twelve or thirteen. It probably depends on the intelligence and sophistication of the audience you're aiming at."

And one more warning: Your imagined biosphere can easily get overly complex. Consider this: Have you ever read a novel of no specific genre in which *every* single animal that exists in the real world is both encountered and described?

Of course not. Billions of animal species live on Earth, from the tiny dust mite on up to the blue whale, and it would follow that a similarly life-harboring world somewhere out in the universe would sustain an enormous number of species as well. Please don't feel as though you have to categorize all of them. Science has so far been unable to do that even here on Earth. So think carefully about what creatures are important to the story at hand. Then either ignore the rest or imply with short cues that there are other things out there, too: a buzzing of unseen insects, something small rattling the underbrush, a shadow passing briefly overhead.

Martin J. Dougherty maintains that "there is plenty of room for conflict and excitement in a world filled with 'people', though some of those might be 'monsters' in the sense of their behavior and values. Monsters are useful, but like any other story element they have to be used judiciously. Monsters that are just fodder for the main characters' egos and swords aren't really serving any useful purpose."

Monsters, as with everything else, can suffer from too much of a good thing. If, for instance, you feel you need a glossary at the end of your book, you're probably doing something wrong. Even though one of my favorite books of all time, *Dune*, has a glossary that covers the world's unique terminology, characters, and place names, it's possible the glossary was added by people who simply underestimated the book's audience. I understood what was going on, who was who, and what was what without it. If you think, *No way are people going to follow this*, stop right there and rewrite all of this, whatever "this" is.

CHAPTER 7

MONSTERS AS METAPHOR

"My zombies are purely a disaster," said George A. Romero, legendary director of *Night of the Living Dead*, in an interview with io9.com[1]. "They are a natural disaster. God has changed the rules, and somehow this thing is happening. My stories are about the humans who deal with it stupidly, and that's what I use them for. I use them to sort of make fun of what's going on in a number of societal events. And that's it, I don't use them to just create gore. Even though I use gore, that's not what my films are about, they're much more political. That's it."

If there is a single answer to why monsters exist in all of the many ways we tell stories, it's that monsters are metaphors. A metaphor is anything that's symbolic or representative of something else, and most often those two things, taken literally, are not really like each other at all. Allegory, closely related, leaves greater room for interpretation on the part of the reader. However subtle or direct, monsters represent ideas, feelings, dangers ... anything an author wants to say.

And this is far from a new or novel idea. Even Sigmund Freud touched on this concept in his 1919 essay "The 'Uncanny'."[2]

> ... an uncanny effect is often and easily produced by effacing the distinction between imagination and reality, such as when something that we have hitherto regarded as imaginary ap-

---

1 io9.com/5851502/why-george-romero-rejected-the-walking-dead-to-make-the-zombie-autopsies
2 "The 'Uncanny'" full text: web.mit.edu/allanmc/www/freud1.pdf

pears before us in reality, or when a symbol takes over the full functions and significance of the thing it symbolizes, and so on. It is this element which contributes not a little to the uncanny effect attaching to magical practices. ... In the midst of the isolation of war-time a number of the English *Strand Magazine* fell into my hands; and, amongst other not very interesting matter, I read a story about a young married couple, who move into a furnished flat in which there is a curiously shaped table with carvings of crocodiles on it. Towards evening they begin to smell an intolerable and very typical odour that pervades the whole flat; things begin to get in their way and trip them up in the darkness; they seem to see a vague form gliding up the stairs—in short, we are given to understand that the presence of the table causes ghostly crocodiles to haunt the place, or that the wooden monsters come to life in the dark, or something of that sort. It was a thoroughly silly story, but the uncanny feeling it produced was quite remarkable.

Although critics of Freud might dismiss his statement "... or when a symbol takes over the full functions and significance of the thing it symbolizes ..." as another example of his tendency to see everything as a metaphor, usually for sex, he's hardly the first or last to make note of that common thread in the nature of the supernatural, including monsters.

J.K. Rowling cast the Dementors as agents first for the Ministry of Magic and then for Voldemort, but don't they also represent depression, or things, thoughts, or events that depress us? Consider this passage from *Harry Potter and the Prisoner of Azkaban.*[3]

"Dementors are among the foulest creatures that walk this earth. They infest the darkest, filthiest places, they glory in decay and despair, they drain peace, hope, and happiness out of the air around them ... Get too near a Dementor and every good feeling, every happy memory will be sucked out of you.

---

3 Arthur A. Levine Books 1999, ©1999 J.K. Rowling

> If it can, the Dementor will feed on you long enough to reduce you to something like itself ... soulless and evil. You will be left with nothing but the worst experiences of your life."

In this case Rowling is playing with the idea that depression begets depression. I think that if you asked most people who actually suffer from depression, they'll be all too familiar with the feeling that "every good feeling, every happy memory" has been "sucked out of" them by the disorder itself. And remember, monsters aren't always about death and predation—some of the scariest monsters are the ones that attack our psychological well being.

Frankenstein's monster and the dinosaurs of *Jurassic Park* are clearly metaphors for the dangers of scientific experimentation into the nature of life—warnings for men not to intrude on God's territory. Both say, "Watch what you're playing with."

Guillermo del Toro told Max Miller in a 2010 Big Think interview[4] that monsters "have multiple values depending on how you use them. They are symbols of great power. I think that at some point, when we became thinking creatures, we decided to interpret the world by creating a mythology of gods and monsters. You know, we created angels, we created demons, we created serpents devouring the moon. We created a mythology to make sense of the world around us.

"And monsters were born at the same time that the angels or any of the beatific creatures and characters were created. ... I am very mindful of the way I deal with them in the movies and in the books because I assign them a specific function and I try to take them to the extreme with that. You know, I make them victims or I make them sympathetic or I make them brutal parasites. And they become a metaphor for something else. Obviously, monsters are living, breathing metaphors."

---

4 "Monsters Are Living, Breathing Metaphors" (bigthink.com/videos/monsters-are-living-breathing-metaphors)

Some monsters, as we'll see in the next few chapters, exist to fill a specific utility in your story. They're agents for the villain, obstacles to be overcome, and so on, but like J.K. Rowling's Dementors, effective monsters work on multiple levels. Some, like Frankenstein's monster, may be obvious symbols of the dangers of science unchecked, while others are more subtle statements that work on a subconscious, allegorical level.

Ask yourself this: Beyond fear, what emotion do I want this monster to elicit in my reader? Or ask: How can this monster play into the theme of my story?

Every story is about something. Some, like George Orwell's *1984*, are overtly political in nature while others, especially the pulp science fiction and fantasy of the Golden Age, are generally less obvious in their politics. Maybe you're writing about something more personal: the nature of love or the journey to overcome grief. So then how does this monster help you express that? Maybe your monster is there, unlike Frankenstein's monster, to exhibit the dangers of limiting scientific inquiry.

An author should always consider the question "Why?" Why is this monster here? And what does it mean? Read on to discover some of the reasons why.

CHAPTER 8

MONSTERS AS OBSTACLES

Sometimes monsters are there simply to get in the way.

In the Norwegian folktale "The Three Billy Goats Gruff," a troll protects a bridge, threatening each of three billy goats who are trying to get to the other side. The first two billy goats trick the troll into waiting for the bigger billy goat to cross—a more satisfying meal, they promise—but in the end it's the third, biggest billy goat that attacks and kills the monster, and all three billy goats end up getting fat off the troll.

That's the more violent, old-school version of the story anyway.

Arguably the three billy goats are as much monsters as the troll, who threatens violence but eventually becomes the victim of it, but as with all obstacles in your story, there's some expectation that the hero will eventually prevail and overcome, one way or another, whatever might be blocking his or her path.

The obstacle is a basic element of storytelling. After all, a story in which our hero plans a trip to the zoo with his family, and everybody's delighted to go, so they do, and they have a great time—the end—is not much of a story. If they go to the zoo and are chased by an escaped tiger, that's a lot more interesting. More exciting still would be if they find a way, using their own resourcefulness, to not only get around the tiger but to recapture it and save the rest of the zoo visitors, too.

In the *Star Trek: Enterprise* episode "Awakening," Captain Archer and Science Officer T'Pol make their way on foot through the Forge, a radioactive desert on T'Pol's homeworld of Vulcan. The radiation defeats their technology, including both communicators and phasers (remember how I mentioned taking away a hero's technology and/or weapons?), which becomes particularly problematic when they encounter a sehlat. A sehlat is a saber-toothed, ursine creature—a particularly ill-tempered predator that chases them up a hill, where Archer and T'Pol are effectively treed. The sehlat is an obstacle they can't seem to get past. They could have stunned it and gone on their way, but that pesky radiation field took away that option.

They're stuck.

Until they are rescued by another Vulcan, that is, who drives the sehlat away. Ultimately, this sequence serves to reinforce the dangers of this Vulcan desert—not only is it radioactive, but it's the hunting grounds of dangerous predatory monsters. But that's not all. The sehlat also plays up Archer and T'Pol's dependence on technology, which later plays into the episode's greater theme of spiritual and political bigotry. And it also allows them to meet this other Vulcan, Arev, who gains their trust by rescuing them from the sehlat and again reinforces that maybe this other, secretive sect of Vulcans have more on the ball than is first thought.

See? That one monster is tied into many, many plot points.

Monsters as obstacles can take any number of forms. The monster may not even have to reveal itself. Sometimes the threat of what might lie between here and there is enough, like Dorothy's mantra "Lions and tigers and bears, oh my!" in *The Wizard of Oz.*

Other times, as David Drake points out, the monster as obstacle doesn't even need to be a living thing. "The Dutch ship-of-the-line in *The Far Side of the World* by Patrick O'Brian fills the same niche as the alien in the movie *Alien.*" Both are there to keep the characters on the run. Both have to be dealt with and overcome at the risk of the characters' life and limb.

As you think about the plot of your story—the conflicts that challenge your characters—you may want to slow them down, speed them up, send them in different directions, force them to work together ... all of these plot points and too many more to list here require obstacles of some kind. Those obstacles can take the form of a bottomless chasm, a character's inability to express his true feelings, or a vicious Vulcan sehlat. Just make sure that the monster—or any obstacle—serves to move your story forward and reveals something about your characters and their attachment to the world around them.

THE MONSTER CREATION FORM: IN WHAT WAY OR WAYS IS IT BETTER OR MORE POWERFUL THAN THE AVERAGE PERSON?

A monster isn't much of an obstacle if you can walk up to it, punch it in the nose, and it falls over dead. Your story should get into the more psychological essence of why it's important for your characters to overcome this monster-obstacle (it's about facing our fear of the unknown, it's a test of resourcefulness when separated from our support structure, and so on). But ultimately there's some kind of physical quality to this thing that's gotten in your characters' way. So what keeps it from getting knocked out with one punch? The questions in this section of the form, from "How big is it?" to "What hurts it?", will go into supporting this statement, but if this monster isn't in some way superior—not in all ways, mind you—to your human characters, it won't work as an obstacle.

CHAPTER 9

MONSTERS AS AGENTS

I'll maintain to my dying day that the scariest monsters in the history of cinema are the flying monkeys in the original 1938 production of *The Wizard of Oz*. Maybe that's because I first saw that movie as a very young child, but these little guys are as creepy as can be. What is it about them? Is it their weird little organ grinder outfits? The batlike wings that are gruesomely unnatural? Their spiky little fangs? The preternatural blue of their fur? Or is it that they serve the Wicked Witch without hesitation, swooping down on Dorothy and her friends from on high and carrying them off? Is this where my fear of heights and flying first started?

If, by the way, your monsters aren't prompting this sort of self-psychoanalysis in your readers, you need to work harder!

My own baggage aside, the concept of monsters as agents, servants, soldiers, etc., is a common and entirely acceptable role for monsters to fill. After all, when the villain sends a mere human after you, you may be able to reason with him, talk him out of it, pay him off ... but a blue, winged monkey that blindly obeys? Good luck.

When considering the introduction of monstrous agents to your story, ask yourself the following four questions.

WHAT TASK NEEDS TO BE DONE?

What does your villain, or for that matter, your hero, need these monster henchmen for? In other words, what role do they actually fill? In the case of the Wicked Witch's flying monkeys, we see them sent out to capture Dorothy and her little dog, too. They fetch things for her, and do it with an unsettling sort of "air superiority" that makes Dorothy and her friends powerless to fend them off.

Ultimately you should answer this question before you even consider monstrous agents. If your story doesn't require them, if there is no mission to be carried out, then forcing them into your story by forcing in a mission for them works against you.

WHY ARE THESE MONSTERS THE RIGHT AGENTS?

You will also have to carefully consider what makes these monsters the right monsters for the job. Living creatures are never perfect, and though life on Earth includes some startling degrees of specialization, most living things tend to be "generalists." We all work to survive—eat, drink, make little creatures, and basically go with the flow. Look at most humans, ant colonies, schools of fish, etc. But some animal societies require some specialists, such as a hive of bees. Some have very unique jobs and that is all they do—the queen only reproduces; the drones are all males, have no stinger, and don't work; and worker bees are all female and have even more specialized jobs such as guards, foragers, undertakers (removing dead bees), etc. So maybe your monster is one of many, a generalist, and is ill-equiped for some specific jobs, or maybe your monster has a unique, singular specialty and is hand-picked for the task.

Either way, remember that while some monsters have special strengths and specialties, they should always be flawed in some way, just as your characters should be. Even monsters that are specifically created by some magical or technological means to serve a specific role won't be literally perfect. If they are, they will make the hero's task a lot harder, or even impossible to overcome, as with Dorothy falling prey to the flying monkeys. Or maybe they are only barely capable, which can show your audience a degree of desperation on the part of your villain.

The Wicked Witch would rather not have to send the flying monkeys on this job, but desperate times call for desperate measures.

HOW ARE THEY CONTROLLED?

Put some thought into how this monster's master manages to control his or her beast, and how the master gained control of the thing in the first place. Those background facts may not make it into the story, but they could be used to keep it moving forward. The means of control, as with pretty much everything having to do with your monsters, your world, and your story, is limited only by your imagination. I would hate to limit that by implying that any one means of control is superior to another.

But if, for instance, the evil wizard controls his minions—let's say they are the animated corpses of giant bears—through the use of an enchanted amulet, that amulet is now "in play" in your story. Do the characters know about this amulet? Can they find out about it along the way? Can they destroy the magic or temporarily interrupt it so the villain no longer has control of his minions? And what happens then? Do these undead giant bears turn on their former master? Is the amulet working to keep them animated so when it turns off they fall over dead? If your hero steals the amulet, will he be able to control the giant undead bears or will they turn on him, or disappear, or freeze up? Is the amulet merely a sort of focus for the evil wizard's own magic, so no matter who's wearing it, he still maintains control of the monsters?

There doesn't have to be a device used to control them, though. Maybe the minions are working for the villain willingly or under some other kind of compulsion. Perhaps the evil wizard is holding their young hostage or is in possession of some artifact or treasure they hope to gain after a period of servitude.

If the monsters have more or less the intelligence of the average dog, they can simply be trained to fill the role. And the humans who interact with them may have to undergo some training as well. Note how Anne

McCaffrey, in *The White Dragon*,[4] keeps a very tight focus on the point of view of the human character Jaxom so we experience what it's like to ride and control a dragon for the first time.

> He felt the bunching of muscle as Ruth assumed a semi-crouch, felt the tension through the back, the shift of musculature under his calves as the huge wings lifted for the all-important first downsweep. Ruth deepened his crouch slightly just as he kicked away from the ground with his powerful hind legs. Jaxom's head snapped on his neck. Instinctively he grabbed for the security of the straps, then hung on tightly as the little white dragon's powerful wing strokes lifted them upward, past the first rank of windows and the startled faces of the holders, up so quickly to the fire-heights that Jaxom saw the other tiers of windows in a blur. Then the great dragons extended their wings, bugling encouragement to Ruth. Fire-lizards swirled about them, adding their silvery voices. Jaxom just hoped they wouldn't startle Ruth or get in his way.

Controlling these beasts can be dangerous for the master, or master-in-training, and if this is the case it can say a lot about your characters, good and evil, and what skills they need to acquire to utilize these minions.

Another element to consider is how your characters interact with their monstrous agents, soldiers, pets, etc., beyond simply controlling them. The Wicked Witch called her flying monkeys "my pretties" and seemed to switch back and forth between talking to a beloved pet and talking to a lower-ranking soldier. The relationship between "master" (or friend, employer, trainer, owner, parent, etc.) and monster agent can and should be as complex as the relationship between any of your characters, or at least between your characters and their most prized possessions. Think about the guy who weeps when the rancor is killed in *Return of the Jedi*. It wasn't a hideous, man-eating monster to him ... but a pet, a friend, a companion.

---

4 Del Rey 1978, ©1978 Anne McCaffrey

WHAT DOES CONTROL OF THIS MONSTER SAY ABOUT THE MASTER?

The mere fact that the villain is able to command an army of monsters, or even just one or a few powerful ones, can be enough to send shivers down your hero's spine. But does the villain control the monster out of desperation and need, or is the villain flexing his or her muscle? In the graphic novel and movie *300*, the heavily fictionalized Xerxes exhibits his overwhelming power by showing off not only the size but the variety of his minions, which include beings such as the Executioner and the Uber Immortal, that can only be described as monsters. The fact that he can control these creatures means he's a force to be reckoned with.

Clark Ashton Smith had a similar idea in mind in his short story "The Double Shadow."

> Not without terror (since man is but mortal) did I, the neophyte, behold at first the abhorrent and tremendous faces of them that obeyed Avyctes. I shuddered at the black writhing of submundane things from the many-volumed smoke of the braziers; I cried in horror at the gray foulness, colossal, without form, that crowded malignly about the drawn circle of seven colors, threatening unspeakable trespass on us that stood at the center. Not without revulsion did I drink wine that was poured by cadavers, and eat bread that was purveyed by phantoms. But use and custom dulled the strangeness, destroyed the fear; and in time I believed implicitly that Avyctes was the lord of all incantations and exorcisms, with infallible power to dismiss the being he evoked.

Sometimes all you have to do is hold the threat of the monster over your opponents' heads, thus creating both the psychological impediment inside the hero when he or she is thinking about this challenge and the physical act of facing the monsters on the field of battle. A villain who can do this to a hero with his monstrous minions is a worthy opponent indeed.

THE MONSTER CREATION FORM: IN WHAT WAY OR WAYS IS IT WEAKER THAN THE AVERAGE PERSON?

This might be as simple as some kind of missing sense: It can hear really well but can't see, for instance. But in the case of this chapter, what is it that makes this monster something that can be used as an "agent" in the first place? It might simply be too stupid to understand it *is* an "agent." Or its master might be using some kind of physical or emotional pain to keep it cowed. One thing most of our heroes would agree on is that there's no force on Heaven or Earth that could compel me to follow the orders of the Grand Vizier of Deathhold, or, say, Adolf Hitler. But some people did, in your story and in real life, so why them and not your hero? What is it about your monster—not just physically but mentally, emotionally, psychologically, spiritually—that makes it weaker than the average person, or, anyway, the hero?

CHAPTER 10

MONSTERS AS SOURCES OF PITY

So far we've focused on what makes monsters scary or dangerous—and we'll continue on that track for much of what follows—but monsters can and should elicit other emotions besides fear or disgust. Maybe our disconnection with the natural order, our confidence that we're the predator and not the prey, allows monsters to work on our emotions the same way animals do. If we're confronted with some snarling beast with obvious ill intentions, our guard goes up, but if that creature reveals its weaknesses and desires, it's possible to get past the initial fear and relate to that creature on a different level.

Mary Shelley does precisely this as the story of Frankenstein's monster unfolds. The more we learn about this creature, the more we begin to see him as a victim of his creator. Consider this excerpt from very near the end of the book, in which the monster finally confronts his own nature and desire for redemption.

> "Oh, it is not thus—not thus," interrupted the being. "Yet such must be the impression conveyed to you by what appears to be the purport of my actions. Yet I seek not a fellow-feeling in my misery. No sympathy may I ever find. When I first sought it, it was the love of virtue, the feelings of happiness and affection with which my whole being overflowed, that I wished to be participated. But now that virtue has become to me a shadow, and

that happiness and affection are turned into bitter and loathing despair, in what should I seek for sympathy? I am content to suffer alone while my sufferings shall endure; when I die, I am well satisfied that abhorrence and opprobrium should load my memory. Once my fancy was soothed with dreams of virtue, of fame, and of enjoyment. Once I falsely hoped to meet with beings who, pardoning my outward form, would love me for the excellent qualities which I was capable of unfolding. I was nourished with high thoughts of honour and devotion. But now crime has degraded me beneath the meanest animal. No guilt, no mischief, no malignity, no misery, can be found comparable to mine. When I run over the frightful catalogue of my sins, I cannot believe that I am the same creature whose thoughts were once filled with sublime and transcendent visions of the beauty and the majesty of goodness. But it is even so; the fallen angel becomes a malignant devil. Yet even that enemy of God and man had friends and associates in his desolation; I am alone."

Your monsters may not be as intelligent as Frankenstein's monster, not quite as able or willing to seek redemption, not as self-aware, but even if it can't express itself as eloquently as this, it may still be able to make its emotional responses clear. Consider this less "intelligent" and direct method of eliciting sympathy.

A slobbering thing, true. Big and grey and, at least in appearance, monstrous. But it had been old and in pain and helpless. She had realized as it sobbed and moaned on that rocky shore as she drove her sword into its quivering flesh that she had been summoned to do this work not because the women of the village feared to kill the creature, but because they pitied it too much.

In that paragraph from the short story "The Cold Step Beyond," author Ian R. MacLeod confronts the issue of a woeful monster by showing us rather than having the creature tell us or have the reader learn of its pitiful state through extended interaction with it. This story also includes a monster slayer capable of the occasional act of sympathetic euthanasia.

And then there's perhaps the most outré movie monster of all, the baby from David Lynch's hypnotic and disturbing *Eraserhead*. This limbless thing—a baby, we are told, but clearly one that frightens even its parents—lays wrapped in swaddling and is both terrifying and pitiful. Even its reluctant parents—along with a confused audience—puzzle over what it is—this sickly, limbless, skinless-looking creature. Its mother at one point shouts, "They're not even sure it *is* a baby!"

And yet, being a baby of *some* sort in need of care, there's a sense of pity, of sorrow, of parental desire to offer comfort even though it is mixed with fear and uncertainty. And it's this ambiguity—*What is this thing? Should we be afraid of it? Should we take care of it?*—that makes it so disturbing. It never attacks, but we're constantly on edge waiting for something else, something even more creepy, to occur.

So when crafting your own monsters, keep their motivations in mind, just as you would a human character, and think of the varied ways they can express those motivations. My dog can't tell me in words how he feels, but he clearly conveys emotions, desires, and so on through nonverbal communication. Does your monster have an impulse to change? A desire for redemption? Is this monstrous agent of the villain only acting in that capacity because the villain is holding something over it? Is this monster attacking because it's trying to protect its young, as does the horta in the classic *Star Trek* episode "The Devil in the Dark?" It could very well be that the way for your heroes to "defeat" the monster is by understanding it, helping it, rescuing it, sending it home ... rather than simply killing it.

THE MONSTER CREATION FORM: WHAT SCARES IT?

Who says the monster always has to be in charge? Some monsters show obvious signs of weakness; for instance, Frankenstein's monster is afraid of fire. But think deeper into this idea. It's a little less obvious than most but can really help bring some depth to your monsters. If your monster is afraid of, say, bright light ... why? Does its unholy master in the Final Pit of the Underblack use bright lights to punish the insubordinate, or does the entrance to the Heavenly Halls, a place inimical to this demon beast's very essence, manifest as a brilliant light? Most complex animals have some set of emotions, some ability to remember and associate. Has this thing been trained, one way or another, to fear ... whatever it is? Making your reader feel at least a little sorry for it can really help breathe life into a beastie.

CHAPTER 11

MONSTERS AS SOURCES OF MAGIC OR TECHNOLOGY

A single monster can serve multiple functions in a story. Monsters as a source of magic or technology can be as threatening as any other superior predator, can inspire pity or other emotions, and can act as agents of either villains or heroes—or both.

In the case of the science fiction classic *Dune*, Frank Herbert created a single monster, the great sandworm, which is perhaps the most "multipurpose" monster ever presented in the genre. Sandworms, a creature hanging on the edge of extinction as a result of human irresponsibility, are an all-in-one metaphor for the fragility of a specialized biosphere. They act as agents of the planet Arrakis's rebellious native population, the Fremen, who ride them into battle against the seat of foreign control of the planet. And we see these sandworms strike, almost blindly, against the human spice miners—as terrifying a mega-predator as we've ever seen.

In other ways, though, the sandworm is a metaphor for the buffalo against a backdrop of the Fremen-as-Native-Americans understory that runs through the series. Though the Fremen are, quite overtly, presented as analogous to the real-world Arab peoples, their approach to this vital animal also conjures memories of the Native Americans. The Fremen don't hunt sandworms, but they do call them, ride them, and harvest their by-products for their own use. The sandworm is as central to Fremen culture as the buffalo was to the Pawnee.

And while the vital spice melange is certainly the sandworm's most sought-after gift —and Herbert's allegory for oil, the vital lifeblood of his universe's single-resource economy— the sandworm's blade-like fangs also serve the Fremen as weapons called crysknives. And the crysknife represents more than a weapon to this highly ritualized society.

> "It is said Duke Leto Atreides rules with the consent of the governed," the Fremen said. "Thus I must tell you the way it is with us: a certain responsibility falls on those who have seen a crysknife." He passed a dark glance across Idaho. "They are ours. They may never leave Arrakis without our consent."[1]

If we keep in mind the broader definition of the word *technology* to mean anything that people make and use for some purpose other than what it might be used for in nature, then a knife made from a giant monster's tooth is as much an example of technology as a smartphone or a starship. Do your fantasy or science fiction characters use the fur or skin of a monster as clothing or shelter? As soon as that hide is in any way altered, it's fair to call it technology.

And though there is no magic, per se, in *Dune*, there is certainly a mystical, mythic, and spiritual nature to the sandworms, at least for the Fremen. The sandworms are, in some ways at least, revered as gods by the Fremen, who approach these monsters as such even when riding them, keeping them above the ground by opening the space between their segments to the abrasive sand.

When thinking about monsters as a source of magic or technology (or both), begin—as always—by asking some basic questions.

WHAT DOES THIS MAGIC OR TECHNOLOGY REPRESENT?

Like oil in our real world, melange in Dune is a symbol of wealth, the essential ingredient to global/interstellar commerce, and a source of cul-

---

1 G.P. Putnam's Sons 1984, ©1965 Frank Herbert

tural and political strife. *Dune*, first published in 1964, is, if anything, even more relevant today as a story of the dangers inherent in a single-resource economy.

Keep in mind that "money" can take on many forms, and for better or worse, tends to be the primary driver of human interaction. Oil equals money; land/real estate equals money. In ancient cultures salt, spices, gold ... all of these resources spurred wars, conquest, exploration—everything humans will do in the name of cold, hard cash.

WHO NEEDS THIS MAGIC OR TECHNOLOGY?

The sandworms of *Dune* are primarily the source of the spice melange and related drugs that serve both the Spacing Guild (as an essential component to the faster-than-light travel upon which the entire interstellar empire depends), and cryptic organizations like the Bene Gesserit (as an equally essential component to their prescient rituals).

It's interesting to consider whether spice made these organizations important to this interstellar society or these important organizations created the need for spice. For the most part, it's easy to answer that sort of chicken-or-the-egg question if only with "they were created together." The demand for oil was fueled by the Industrial Revolution, but that revolution would have withered on the vine had we not discovered this rich energy source—or had someone stopped to consider its considerable downsides.

WHY DOES THIS MAGIC OR TECHNOLOGY REQUIRE THIS MONSTER?

Answering this question may be as easy as tying the result inextricably to the cause. In *Dune*, the sandworms create the spice. Frank Herbert makes that relationship clear and, at least in this first book of the series, insurmountable.

> "Few products escape the CHOAM touch," the Duke said, "Logs, donkeys, horses, cows, lumber, dung, sharks, whale fur—the most prosaic and the most exotic ... even our poor pundi rice

from Caladan. Anything the Guild will transport, the art forms of Ecaz, the machines of Richesse and Ix. But all fades before melange. A handful of spice will buy a home on Tupile. It cannot be manufactured, it must be mined on Arrakis. It is unique and it has true geriatric properties."

It seems to be some cosmic imperative that the most valuable resources also have to be the most difficult to find. Look at the lengths the oil companies go to find and tap new sources of oil. In *Dune*, melange is excreted by sandworms. It just sits on the surface waiting to be scooped up, but the machines used to gather it create vibrations that attract sandworms that attack those mining operations with potentially devastating results.

Human agriculture is a great example of the myriad uses we're able to draw from a single animal. But if you're getting leather from a domesticated cow, that's not the same thing as extracting a crysknife from a wild sandworm. Monsters, by definition, provide us with a greater challenge than domesticated animals. Like the spice/sandworm relationship in *Dune*, the monster-derived resource is valuable due to the difficulty in gathering it.

HOW IS THIS MAGIC OR TECHNOLOGY HARVESTED FROM THE MONSTER?

The larval form of Frank Herbert's sandworms, known as sandtrout, are a source of a more potent form of the spice melange. When the sandtrout are introduced to water, then squeezed, a highly concentrated form of the drug is released, and it's this highly concentrated spice that is most prized by the Bene Gesserit.

Because Arrakis is a desert planet and water is as precious and rare a commodity there as melange is to the rest of the universe, the sacrifice of water to produce this drug is a significant expense. Likewise it's the sandtrout that leach water from the planet, allowing their adult forms, the sandworms, to enjoy the dry environment in which they thrive. Again, Herbert presents a case for the balancing effect of a biosphere, in which life forms are inherently connected to their environment and even change that environment to suit their own survival.

Do your characters have to kill this rare monster in order to gather its mana for use in magical rituals? Or can this monster and your heroes somehow find a balance, as the Fremen have with the sandworms? If you pull the fang from a dragon to use it as an indestructible magic sword, will the dragon grow another? Or will it die in the process? How limited and dangerous are these magical resources?

It's that balance between rarity and the difficulty of gathering it that can make your monster-derived magic either rare and precious or inexpensive and ubiquitous.

CHAPTER 12

BRINGING OUT THE GOOD AND EVIL IN PEOPLE

Who is the villain of *Night of the Living Dead*?

As we've already heard from director George A. Romero, it isn't the monsters.

Consider the zombie horde. Zombies aren't villains as we've defined them in this book—they're simply there, wandering through the countryside or empty city streets. The fact that they're the animated corpses of people, some even people you know and love (or knew and loved, as it stands) and that they're actively trying to eat you makes them even more terrifying. But the classic zombie—in the style of *Night of the Living Dead*, which we've seen in zombie stories from *The Walking Dead* to *World War Z*—has very little or no intelligence and no real desire beyond simply feeding.

What zombies really do is put people in peril, and then it's up to the people—the living people—to figure out how they're going to react to that problem. Romero described his zombies as a natural disaster, and that comparison is apt. We see this in reality. We've all heard stories of heroism that occur during actual natural disasters like floods or tornados—the guy who crawls through the rubble and finds the neighbor lady's dog, and everyone cheers and we get a chance to feel better about humanity, and ourselves in the process.

Then there were the reports of rapes, looting, murders, and assaults during Hurricane Katrina. Similar reports crop up during other natural and man-made disasters. Sometimes these disasters bring out the worst in people. The city's been destroyed, there seems to be a breakdown in law and order, so we're just going to go crazy. The earthquake—or the zombie apocalypse—becomes an excuse for the worst of our human behaviors to rise to the surface.

Monsters can bring out the good in people by encouraging them to react in some heroic way—*Let's get everybody together to save our culture, save what's good about us.* Or they can bring out the evil, with people who think, *How do I take advantage of this?* The clash between these good and bad reactions is often where the conflict arises in zombie stories.

Then there's the third option, which is likely the terrain of your tertiary characters, the people who are so terrified, so out of their element, that they can't see past the practical need to protect themselves, to live through the night. These characters add yet another danger element to those struggling to survive this unexpected calamity.

Like a hurricane, zombies and many other monsters are just there, and how they got there and why—like Alfred Hitchcock's notoriously unexplained avian invasion in *The Birds*—isn't what the story is really about. There are hints in the original *Night of the Living Dead* that some kind of comet caused this zombie plague, but that goes by fast, is never verified, and in the end, who cares? At least right now we're more concerned with living through the night than figuring out how it happened. Even later movies in the series, like the underappreciated *Day of the Dead*, confront the lack of success that science had in determining why the recently deceased got up and started eating people. And this only heightens the frightening nature of the zombies. They aren't just a natural disaster, they're an as-yet unknown natural disaster that no one was able to predict, let alone prevent or cure.

Another thing that makes the zombie apocalypse so unsettling, and thereby makes heroism in the face of it much harder, is the seeming unending nature of it. Going into a burning building to save the cat represents a single short-lived act of heroism. You either save the cat or not, and soon enough the fire department will put out the fire or the building will burn to the ground. Either way, this disaster ends. But the zombie apocalypse—or the invasion of your own original monsters—can go on and on, possibly forever. No matter what, your characters are always in danger. They can never just go outside and go about their normal lives in any way without being in at least some danger of being attacked by zombies or those seeking to take advantage of the situation.

This idea is at the heart of AMC's television adaptation of the comic book series *The Walking Dead*. We're seeing heroes like father, husband, and police officer Rick Grimes and villains like the Governor, the would-be dictator of his little walled-off town, struggle with how they can go on in the face of never-ending disaster. Both are looking for a place of safety, and both lead a group of survivors trying to regain some semblance of a normal life after the total collapse of human civilization. Rick and the Governor go about that same goal in very different ways—and immediately come into conflict with each other. Meanwhile, the zombies are more than happy to take a bite out of both.

Bringing out the good and evil in your characters is hardly limited to the zombie apocalypse. Virtually any monster can do that. If you've trapped a cast of characters in an isolated locale and thrown even a single monster at them, those characters will naturally rise to their own overriding impulses, whether that impulse is to protect everyone else at all costs or to protect himself at all costs.

Keep in mind, too, that monsters can bring out more than simply "good" and "evil" in your characters. It's often difficult to clearly define those two words. Going back to *The Walking Dead*, neither hero Rick nor villain the Governor are entirely good or entirely evil. In fact, both men are deeply damaged and trying to lead their respective groups of survivors to the best of their ability. Both make terrible mistakes, are forced into tough decisions, and reveal moments of both compassion and violence.

And yet one is clearly the villain, and one is the hero.

I define a villain as someone whose motivations you understand but whose methods you abhor, and a hero as someone whose motivations you understand and whose methods you admire. In the same way that monsters can bring about this split in method, they can also bring out the resourcefulness in people—and both Rick and the Governor have proven themselves to be quite resourceful. Your monsters can allow your characters to exhibit qualities like tenacity, loyalty, trustworthiness, a capacity for forgiveness, and so on. All of these characteristics are brought to the forefront by placing characters in a world full of monsters that force them to act, choose, and become something more (or, tragically, less) than they were before the story began.

German philosopher Friedrich Nietzsche wrote, "Whoever fights monsters should see to it that in the process he does not become a monster. And if you gaze long enough into an abyss, the abyss will gaze back into you."

In some cases, there are monsters you can only defeat by becoming a monster yourself or, as is the case with the science fiction film *Pitch Black*, by embracing the monster within. In this story, Riddick changes from fellow monster into unexpected hero—yet he's still the dangerous man he always was. The movie begins with dire warnings about the villainous Riddick, a sort of supervillain in custody on his way to a prison planet. Once the monsters—this alien planet's indigenous predators—make their presence known, Riddick at first acts in his own self-interest, but eventually he's compelled to take sides and finds his inner hero while the bounty hunter who won't set aside his beef with Riddick becomes the story's true villain. Meanwhile the monsters are just hungry, and Riddick's reviled, violent tendencies become celebrated, vital skills.

Dark Horse Comics editor-in-chief Scott Allie says, "To me it's not just about the good or evil in the human characters, but more nuanced qualities. Stories can explore whether protagonists are good or not, but that's so broad. I'm more interested in whether they're honest or loyal or vain and in how that manifests."

Or as Iain M. Banks wrote in *Against a Dark Background*, "We are a race prone to monsters ... and when we produce one we worship it."[1]

---

1 *Against a Dark Background* by Iain M. Banks (1993)

GREAT MONSTERS: GODZILLA

Star of twenty-eight films and counting, at least one animated TV series, books, comic books, video games, and other media, Godzilla has earned his title as "King of the Monsters." This giant radioactive dinosaur-beast was first seen in director Ishiro Honda's 1954 film *Gojira*—a mash-up for the Japanese words for gorilla and whale, hinting at an early concept for the beloved monster that thankfully didn't survive to the final cut. The bleak and more overtly political *Gojira* was recut for American audiences as *Godzilla*.

Having been created by atomic mutation, imbued with massive size and the ability to exhale a sort of radioactive fire, Godzilla is a blatant metaphor for all the evils of the nuclear age. And as such it should come as no surprise that this creature both comes from, and most frequently targets, Japan.

In a country still reeling from the atomic bomb attacks on Hiroshima and Nagasaki, Japan knew all too well the danger of nuclear weapons, but it's difficult not to see Godzilla as a secondary allegory tied closely to the (possibly apocryphal) quote attributed to Japanese Admiral Yamamoto after his successful attack on Pearl Harbor: "I fear all we have done is to awaken a sleeping giant and fill him with a terrible resolve."

Atomic tests awaken Godzilla, stirring him up from the depths of the ocean. He unleashes widespread destruction eerily reminiscent of the bombing of Tokyo and other Japanese cities, including Hiroshima and Nagasaki, in World War II.

But like many monsters (maybe even all), Godzilla helps us regain some power over the things that make us feel most powerless. If we can defeat Godzilla, we have defeated the A-bomb.

Many monsters sub in for this sort of real-world evil—for example, the alien invaders in *Invasion of the Body Snatchers* represented the threat of communism to a Cold War–era America.

As Godzilla's career progressed, he began to take on the unlikely role of hero, protecting the Earth from one monstrous invader after another. In the surprisingly emotional *Son of Godzilla*, viewers see both harried parent and confused child as a source of pity. Oh, and he has a cheeky sense of humor to boot—at least in the later films.

But hero or villain, the idea for Godzilla spawned from our own irresponsibility, our own insatiable appetite for war, destruction, and ever more powerful weapons, but he brings with him all the human qualities of redemption, forgiveness, and even parental love.

The giant monster, or *kaiju*, has become a staple in Japanese science fiction and has significant audience appeal in the United States as well. Guillermo del Toro's successful *Pacific Rim* is case in point, not to mention the new *Godzilla* reboot.

The giant monster can be a bit of a writing challenge. Its threat and effects are more widespread and less personal. Still, a giant monster, like a zombie horde, can be seen as a force of nature, and how the puny human characters react to its sudden appearance and the violent destruction of their city is where the story really rests.

ARCHETYPES: VAMPIRES

Time and again I've half-joked that I'd like to call for a United Nations Resolution establishing a global ten-year moratorium on any new vampire stories—the poor old bloodsucker is just that tired. Who could possibly have anything fresh or interesting to say about it?

Then I read the graphic novel and saw the movie *30 Days of Night* and thought, *Okay, there's the last of the really interesting, original vampire stories. Moratorium starts now.*

Then I saw the brilliantly scary and affecting movie *Let Me In*, and the moratorium was delayed yet again.

And the fact that vampires are as popular as ever, regardless of my opinion on this vampire story or that vampire film, means that at least in this case, you can't listen to me.

What both *30 Days of Night* and *Let Me In* did—as well as some other vampire stories like the brilliant Octavia E. Butler's *Fledgling*, the action thriller *Underworld*, and even Stephenie Meyer's mega-best-selling Twilight series—is take the accepted vampire archetype and tweak it a little. None of these new vampire stories bear much resemblance to Bram Stoker's *Dracula*. We'll discuss the concept of cliché vs. archetype a little later, but for now I think it's clear that the vampire has taken on quite a wide variation in forms over the years, and your vampires can be as different from anyone else's as your imagination and story demand.

But what is it that accounts for the enduring nature of the vampire myth? What keeps drawing us back to this monster? Author Chelsea Quinn Yarbro, creator of the vampire hero the Comte de Saint-Germain, introduced in her novel *Hotel Transyl-*

vania, has thought about that quite a bit. "It's tempting to say that their enduring popularity is part of their semi-immortality, but that is too facile. Vampires have immunized themselves against death, and many of us from time to time would like to be able to do that. And vampires, in [their] need [for] close physical association with the living in order to survive, stir up all kinds of erotic responses. It's a winning combination."

Clearly vampires act on a metaphorical or allegorical level. Were the original vampire myths inspired by the selfishness and recklessness of European aristocracy? It's common idiom to refer to certain members of the privileged class as bloodsuckers. These are people who have set themselves apart from ordinary citizens and live in a separate world in the same way that vampires exist at night and the rest of us live in the daylight. These are people who feed off the labor—the blood—of the peasantry.

Vampires in their various iterations have been quite effective in bringing out the good and evil in others. In Bram Stoker's seminal vampire novel, *Dracula*, poor Renfield easily succumbs to Dracula's power and becomes a twisted servant of the count (note that aristocratic title—hardly an accident). But Jonathan Harker manages to survive similar treatment. He rises to the occasion and proves to be one of the heroes of the story. In many ways, vampires force us to choose between servitude or resistance.

Even then, vampires are occasionally portrayed as victims in their own right, lovelorn lost souls wrapped in guilt and regret, who seek release from their eternal torment even as they drain the blood of the locals. And plenty of other authors, as Chelsea

Quinn Yarbro points out, have presented them as objects of love, or at least lust.

When I asked Scott Allie of Dark Horse Comics to pick the scariest monster he's ever come across, he said, "That little Glick boy in 'Salem's Lot. The miniseries was great, but the book is the thing I go back to year after year to get terrified all over again. Nothing else does that for me. Stephen King set up Danny Glick emotionally for us, made us care so much about Danny's friend Mark Petrie, and made us identify so much with the scene in which Danny is floating outside Mark's bedroom window, scratching to get in. He has such a talent for making everything seem real, utterly convincing, and as a kid, and then a teen, and so on, I really believed Danny could be outside my window. The little boy scared the hell out of me. Still does."

REAL MONSTERS: MOTHER NATURE

In an effort to find a reference to a tornado that's referred to as a "monster," I entered the words "monster tornado" into Google and it came back with more than twenty-seven million results. What else would we call something that descends on us from the sky and destroys everything in its path?

If Godzilla or a zombie horde are the monster equivalent of a natural disaster, what about the natural disaster as a monster then? It's certainly a device to consider, unless Syfy's *Sharknado* has thoroughly salted that earth. For what it's worth, I don't think it has.

Stephen King's novella *The Mist* begins with what appears to be an unusual weather phenomenon: A strange fog bank descends over the town of Bridgton, Maine. In a way the mist itself is as much a monster in that story as the Lovecraftian horrors it hides. It's something that you can't stop, can't predict, and can't fight—and in a very real sense it acts in collusion with a panoply of dangerous outsider predators.

"Nature is scary, but in an abstract and not always apparent way," says author Martin J. Dougherty. "This subtle threat is easy to forget about, even though it creates so many other threats that make for moments of real horror ..."

So then, is Mother Nature a monster hiding in plain sight? Nature is all well and good when it's sunny and warm outside, but when the dark clouds descend, the world around you transforms into a destructive force: a monster.

Nina Hess cautions that nature as monster is "difficult to do right, but it's a fantastic antagonist—and you don't have to over-analyze that antagonist's motives." Like the zombie, a tornado (with or without sharks) isn't thinking. It isn't plotting against you, but it will eat you just the same.

THE CRYPTIDS: THE LOCH NESS MONSTER

The first widely circulated report of a sighting of an unexplained monster in Scotland's Loch Ness came from a vacationing couple by the name of Spicer. The couple claimed to have had a near miss with what came to be called "Nessie," as the beast shambled across a lakeside road. That was July of 1933, and people have been reporting sightings of something in Loch Ness ever since.

Loch Ness is a long, relatively thin body of water, twenty-four miles in length and almost eight-hundred feet deep. Geologists believe the freshwater lake was connected to the ocean millions of years ago. Could a small breeding population of plesiosaurs, dinosaurs that swam Earth's oceans until the mass extinction sixty-six million years ago, have found their way into Loch Ness and lived on?

Animals believed to be extinct at some time have been later discovered alive, but something as big as a plesiosaur is a lot different than a particular kind of algae or even the odd deepwater fish. These real-life monsters were fifty feet long or more.

Over the decades the number of serious attempts to find the Loch Ness Monster have been eclipsed by the various theories offered to either explain away the sightings or to explain why there haven't been more sightings. Was it that these witnesses just saw a floating log? A boat wake? Or maybe what they saw was a school of salmon?

In the meantime, stories and myths continue to spread. And Nessie isn't alone out there. Dozens of lakes around the world are known for similar sightings, which prompted the creation of a whole category of cryptids known simply as lake monsters.

If science can be certain of anything it's that plenty of individual animal species still have not yet been properly identified and categorized. And the waters of Loch Ness are deep and murky. Could it be there's something down there, perhaps hiding in some secret aquatic cave?

Monsters come from the dark places, and a remote Scottish loch nearly a thousand feet deep could certainly be described as a dark place. Contrary to our definition of "monster," however, is the fact that Nessie doesn't seem to mean anyone harm. In fact, Nessie tends to inspire warmer feelings. She's become the loch's official mascot, a boon to local tourism rather than a hindrance, and the only reason people outside of that part of Scotland have ever heard of the place. Modern sightings of Nessie are rarely described as particularly frightening, and the monster's behavior overall is not threatening. This reclusive beast doesn't attack boats or people ... unless you add that part to your own version of the legend.

This begs the question: Is your creation a monster (the Loch Ness Monster), has it simply become an animal (a plesiosaur), or does it fall into a third category: mascot, friend, or pet (Nessie)? This is a distinction you'll want to put some thought into. In the first instance, the Loch Ness Monster is a nightmare creature, purely a monster that challenges your characters, probably physically. The middle category ends the relevance of a word like *monster* and makes the plesiosaur's story one of survival against all odds. And then there's Nessie, who would be equally at home in a Saturday morning cartoon as it would be in that cold Scottish loch.

Like dragons, vampires, or unicorns, lake monsters are wide open for the taking. What could the reclusive descendant of the Jurassic ocean's top predator represent for you? The fact that there are still unexplored places on this planet? Or that it's possible that more than this one species of dinosaur survived into contemporary times and more live in that cave down there?

A lake, river, or sea monster can also be an effective obstacle: We have to cross this body of water, rumored to be the home of a mysterious and terrifying monster. A little research into the lore surrounding the world's lake monsters can generate all sorts of inspiration for similar beasts. You may even want to consider showing your characters responding to the threat of the lake monster, but later discovering that either no such thing exists or it's not nearly as threatening as your characters believed.

As with Bigfoot, we're still waiting for evidence of a real animal, so in the meantime we're left with the imaginary monster, which is good enough for me. The Loch Ness Monster is as much yours as anyone's, but use it carefully!

MONSTROUS THINGS: CURSED ITEMS

Cursed items can take any number of forms, from the infamous *Necronomicon* of H.P. Lovecraft's stories (and referenced in many other works since) to the animate ritual doll of television's equally infamous *Trilogy of Terror*. The movie version of *The Exorcist* (and a couple of its sequels) even hinted that the demon or demons that eventually found their way into the little girl's body came from some artifact snuck out of an archeological dig in the Holy Land. The collected fantasy and horror lore is full of cursed items, including the Brady boys' brush with a tarantula (courtesy of a taboo tiki doll) in that famous Hawaii episode of *The Brady Bunch*.

Richard Baker, award-winning game designer and best-selling author of *Condemnation*, says, "Cursed items suggest an element of choice—at some point the victim chooses his fate. Something like the monkey's paw or the Lemarchand puzzle box from *Hellraiser* doesn't destroy you if you have the wisdom or innocence to leave it alone."

The cursed item as a way to summon or unleash a monster is so common it was one of the first things lampooned in the revisionist monster movie *The Cabin in the Woods*. Different monsters are ready to make their presence known, depending on what cursed item the subjects choose from the mysterious collection in the cabin's basement.

And if in the brief course of this examination we can leap from *The Brady Bunch* to *Hellraiser* in only two moves, it surely means, as Lynn Abbey suggests, that an author "would find it easiest to conjure up a story about a cursed item. There's an infinite number of items in the universe and an infinite number of curses, which would give me infinity-squared potential stories."

PART III

HOW TO WRITE THEM

This is where the rubber meets the road—or more appropriately, where pen meets paper. Now that you know what monsters are and why you need or want them in your story, the rest of this book will cover practical advice on how to create monsters, how to reveal them over time, and how to describe them and their actions in a compelling fashion.

Alongside the advice to follow, the best classroom for writing monsters, and "writing scary" in general, is carefully reading and rereading the stories and novels that have scared you in the past. I like to go back to *The Hot Zone* by Richard Preston. Even though this is a nonfiction book and the "monster" in question is the very real Ebola virus, this book has the scariest first chapter I've ever read. Preston's vivid, unflinching, and entirely human description of what it's like to die from Ebola makes that little bug the scariest monster in the history of the written word—maybe more so because it's real.

Always think about *how this monster moves your story forward*. How does it make your story more interesting, how does it play into the core conflict of the tale, and what makes it personal to your characters? Is it something they find frightening or pitiable, or even useful? Don't try to build a story around a monster; build a monster from within your story.

Or, as author David Drake says, "I don't define the monster. The situation defines the monster: You create the sort of monster that the situation requires."

CHAPTER 13

SETTING THE RULES

In the introduction to this book (remember way back then?) we discussed the difference between realism and plausibility, and here's where we put that to the test.

What makes one dragon "realistic" and another "unrealistic" when both are entirely fictional creatures?

The answer is that one operates within a set of clearly defined and consistently applied rules, and the other doesn't.

Fantasy, science fiction, and horror books, movies, and games are sold on the basis that they are wildly original alternate realities, and it comes as no surprise to anyone that there's magic, weird locales, bizarre beings, or terrifying monsters in any of them. The fact is that fans of these genres want to believe in these worlds—which is to say they're not just willing to suspend their disbelief, they're depending on it. But the biggest and most damaging complaint you'll get from genre fans is that something you've done drops them out of the story and makes them think in concrete, realistic terms when they should be temporarily living in a strange fantasy world, distant future universe, or haunted house.

Your readers or viewers are coming in with the desire to be complicit in the fantasy and will happily accept every little weird detail until it's built into an effective, plausible creature. It's entirely up to you to set the rules, and the fact is those rules are limited only by your imagination. There is no such thing as "too weird." Your readers don't believe the monster is real; they believe that it's real in that world. As such, consistency is paramount.

Author Martin J. Dougherty agrees that "there has to be a set of rules, though you don't have to reveal them all to the reader. I tend to mentally pigeonhole monsters with a stereotype: 'crazed rampaging giant stompy thing' or 'inimical disembodied force' and then if I want a particular ability I try to justify it in terms of both feasibility that the monster could have that power and also what the reader has seen it do."

"What the reader has seen it do" is at the heart of the point. Your readers only know as much about that monster as you show (not tell) them. "If a monster needs the power of having resistance to cold," Dougherty says, "that's fine, so long as it's not come up before, but if two hundred pages ago it was shivering on a glacier, then it can't have that power now. Not without a glacier-removal rewrite."

Which leads me to the next point: Always be open to change.

Until the book is published or the movie or game is released, no one has seen that monster of Martin Dougherty's freezing on a glacier. While you're still writing and your story demands that the monster have that resistance to cold, go back and revise accordingly.

RULES FOR CREATION

Richard Baker's personal rule of thumb is that a good monster needs "an offense, a defense, and a utility feature.

"Offense is obvious—what's it going to do to you? Claw you to pieces? Stick you with a proboscis and suck out your insides? Feast on your psyche? Ideally it should be a fate that fills the reader or viewer with visceral dread. Defense means simply, why is it hard to kill? Monsters shouldn't be a problem you can solve easily with whatever firearm happens to be handy. It could be there are a lot of the monsters, and you're likely to run out of bullets before you deal with them all. Finally, utility means something not directly related to killing or surviving that adds interesting story elements. For example, the Blair Witch marks her territory with disturbing little stick figures and makes people stand in the corner before she kills them. Vampires can't enter a home without being invited. That sort of thing."

It's hardly a coincidence that Richard Baker spends a lot of his time designing role-playing games (RPGs) like *Dungeons & Dragons* and the upcoming *Primeval Thule* campaign setting. In order to provide a consistent play experience, RPG monsters have to be expressed with a set of game terms. This can help very clearly define what a monster can and can't do, but just because there's a set of game rules around a creature doesn't necessarily make it plausible. The maker of that monster still has to have a solid story purpose in mind. The monster, for instance, has to make sense coming from that specific alien environment, and so on. You can pick up some valuable tips and a whole lot of inspiration from the various role-playing games.

Take, for example, the Star-thing of Nheb from *Primeval Thule*.[1]

STAR-THING OF NHEB CR 9

Pallid and slimy, this hulking creature stands almost 10 feet tall. Its flesh is oddly translucent, as if it is not entirely solid in this plane of existence, and its arms each end in three powerful, coiling tentacles.

XP 6,400
NE Large aberration
INIT +1; **SENSES** blindsight 60 ft.; Perception +16

---

1 Star-Thing of Nheb ©2013 Sasquatch Game Studio LLC, used by permission.

DEFENSE

AC 21, touch 9, flat-footed 21 (–1 size, +12 natural)

HP 104 (11d8 + 55)

FORT +9, Ref +3, Will +11

IMMUNE cold, disease, poison

OFFENSE

SPEED 30 ft., swim 20 ft.

MELEE 2 tentacles +14 (2d6+7 and grab)

SPELL-LIKE ABILITIES (CL 11th)

constant—mind blank

1/day—rainbow pattern (DC 16), teleport

3/day—blur, dimensional anchor (+7 ranged touch), dispel magic

SPECIAL ATTACKS constrict (2d6+7 and life drain)

STATISTICS

STR 25, **DEX** 10, **CON** 19, **INT** 12, **WIS** 15, **CHA** 8

BASE ATK +8; **CMB** +16 (+20 grapple); **CMD** 26

FEATS Great Fortitude, Improved Overrun, Improved Natural Attack (tentacle), Iron Will, Power Attack, Toughness

SKILLS Climb +21, Escape Artist +14, Knowledge (arcana) +15, Perception +16, Stealth +14

LANGUAGE understands but does not speak Common

ECOLOGY

ENVIRONMENT cold mountains

ORGANIZATION solitary or band (2–4)

TREASURE standard

SPECIAL ABILITIES

ETHEREAL SHIFT (SU) A star-thing can shift from the Material Plane to the Ethereal Plane as a move action (or part of a move action). It can take a grabbed creature with it, but if the grapple ends while the grabbed creature is ethereal, the grabbed creature returns to the Material Plane. A star-thing can only remain ethereal for a number of rounds equal to 1 + its Con modifier (5 rounds typically) and then must return. It cannot use this ability again for 2 rounds per round it was shifted into the Ethereal plane. The ability is otherwise similar to ethereal jaunt (CL 15th).

LIFE DRAIN (SU) A creature constricted by a star-thing's tentacles takes 1d4 Constitution drain (Fortitude save DC 19 negates). The star-thing heals 5 damage for every point of Constitution it drains.

Star-things are hideous, shambling monstrosities alien to this world. They generally reside in desolate mountain heights, preferring the cold temperatures and rarefied air of the highest peaks. While star-things appear to be huge, horrible alien beasts, they are actually quite intelligent. They have been known to lure invaders to their dooms by mesmerizing them with dancing auroras of eerie witch-lights. Star-things are especially tenacious foes, and often go to great lengths to hunt down enemies who manage to escape them.

Star-things are inscrutable and incommunicative, but are known to seek out deposits of rare minerals or places of ancient power. While star-things have little use for humans or other terrestrial beings of any sort, powerful (or foolhardy) spellcasters or cultists have occasionally trafficked with the creatures by bribing them with the rare minerals they seek or the lost artifacts of their race. In the service of someone who knows how to bargain with it, a star-thing can be a peculiarly horrible and effective assassin.

A lot of these game terms can be hard to sort out if you aren't familiar with the D20 system or role-playing games in general, so you might not understand what a speed of thirty feet means. But in general, the higher the number the more powerful, bigger, and better it is. Believe me, I am *not* suggesting that before you write your fantasy novel you have to design the role-playing game. But do consider expressing the creature's abilities in terms of comparison to something real. So maybe this monster is twice as strong as the average man, can climb like a leopard, and is as comfortable in cold conditions as a polar bear.

THE MONSTER CREATION FORM: HOW DOES IT MOVE?

A star-thing can "shift from the Material Plane to the Ethereal Plane as a move action (or part of a move action)." How does your monster move? Does it swim, walk, climb like a spider, fly, "shift" from one dimension to another, or teleport via magical or psychic means, simply disappearing in one place and reappearing somewhere else? Humans walk on two legs and have close contact with animals (like dogs and cats) that walk on four legs, but things with more legs (spiders, insects) or no legs at all (snakes) kinda freak us out. It's also easier for us to understand how to at least fend off a monster if we have a sense of how fast and agile it is, but what if it can just *appear* behind you? The Weeping Angels of *Doctor Who* are one of TV's most terrifying monsters. They can only move when you're not looking at them, so you have to keep your eyes open and on them, literally every second—and that's not easy to do!

There's more than one flavor of fantasy and lots of different approaches to science fiction, and what might be plausible in one sub-genre may be implausible in another. So-called "hard" science fiction, for instance, has a readership that expects more scientific rigor in all its various imagined elements, from how a starship works to how a monster has evolved into the thing it is. Thinking about a creature in terms of its native environment—this alien planet's gravity, temperature, radiation, geology, etc.—can be an interesting thought experiment, and one that can guide you in the creation of a more plausible creature.

I like to look at science fiction as a ratio of science to fiction. How you weight that ratio is entirely up to you. There's an audience out there for all iterations. Something like *Star Wars* weights that ratio way more in favor of fiction—say, nine parts fiction to one part science. Authors like Arthur C. Clarke, Isaac Asimov, and Greg Bear, on the other hand, tend to write books that are more like nine parts science to one part fiction, like Bear's *Darwin's Radio*. That said, your monsters are still your monsters, and you are their creator.

And then there's fantasy, which is, by definition, the place where anything can happen. If you're creating the world from the ground up, you have to set all of the rules—not just the rules for monsters. How big is a dragon in your fantasy setting? How big do you want it to be? Maybe they sit on your characters' shoulders, or maybe the entire world is a dragon and we all live inside it or build our cities on its back. You tell me!

But once you tell me—or better yet, show me—stick to the rules you've set ... whatever they may be.

CHAPTER 14

SIZE

When I asked author and editor Brendan Deneen which he thinks is scarier, big monsters or small monsters, he responded, "Nah, as we all know, size doesn't matter! One of my favorite movie monsters is Chucky. Another is Godzilla. Hmm ... Chucky vs. Godzilla ... let's make that happen!"

I'll leave that one for Brendan to pitch, but I agree wholeheartedly with his original assertion: Size doesn't matter, since both large monsters and small are scary in their own right.

BIG IS SCARY

As animals go, we humans are actually really big. Sure, there are some land animals that are bigger—like elephants or giraffes—and plenty more in the oceans, up to and including the blue whale, which can grow in excess of ninety-eight feet in length. But rest assured, the list of animals that are bigger than the average adult human is a lot shorter than the list of animals that are smaller than we are.

Still, enormous creatures put us on guard. Even among human populations, might has often meant right. In a time when physical strength was a significant survival tool, the biggest, strongest member of the tribe likely led the communal group. It has taken us a very long time as a species to get to the current state in which "geeks" like Bill Gates win by capitalizing on their brains and creativity. And even now, more primitive and retrograde human societies, like high schools, still tend to be the kingdom of the biggest kid.

Big monsters tend to rely on physical intimidation and mass destruction. It would be difficult to stand in the path of Godzilla, look up, and not be afraid. Would that enormous beast even see you? It could squash you without even realizing it.

When creating giant monsters, think about what that size differential means to your characters. For instance, is there a thread in your story that has to do with characters working through some sort of psychological baggage? Has a character felt physically intimidated by a bigger person and overcomes that trauma by defeating the even bigger, more intimidating giant monster? Has the skinny, smart guy cooked up a high-tech weapon that neutralizes Zorgloth the Living Asteroid, after all the hulking super soldiers have failed, and proven once and for all that intellectual strength, not physical strength, is most valuable?

And how big is big enough to intimidate? Bigger than a human? Or just bigger than the real-life creature? The answer: whatever is scary enough to frighten your characters.

Take insects and spiders for example. The way they breathe and the amount of oxygen they need limits their size. Millions of years ago, when the atmosphere contained a much higher concentration of oxygen, insects were quite a bit bigger. *Brontoscorpio anglicus* was a scorpion that lived about four hundred million years ago and is estimated to have been three feet long. But that was then, and this is now. A scorpion that big couldn't get enough oxygen into its body in our atmosphere, thankfully. This simple fact makes giant insects difficult to justify in a science fiction environment. Of course in a fantasy world, where a monster's real-world anatomy or the chemical composition of the atmosphere might be easier to dismiss or work around, you can easily imagine scorpions a hundred feet long. But whether it's a hundred feet long or three feet, that's one big scorpion, and few characters would have the courage to tackle it.

Another thing to consider is how great size tends to affect the rest of the creature's physical makeup. Really big animals tend to be a little slow, their feet (like an elephant's) are wider, and their legs are more like columns than spikes.

For science fiction monsters, the combination of a high-oxygen atmosphere and a low surface gravity can result in all sorts of mammoth flying insects, whereas a high-gravity planet with a corrosive atmosphere might be home to a bunch of squat, shelled creatures.

When writing giant monsters, try to describe their size in relation to other things the character and reader might know. In fantasy, it tends to come off as anachronistic if characters are commenting on the size and weight of a monster in concrete terms. "It was 316 feet long and weighed 1,204 tons" doesn't sound like something a resident of a medieval fantasy world would say. The same description in a science fiction story can be plausible, though, if it's the result of some kind of sensor scan.

If the giant slime-beast in your fantasy story is described as twice as tall as the king's watchtower, and we've previously seen the king walk up twenty flights of stairs to get to the top of that tower, we now know this monster is the size of a twenty-story building, without a character actually having to implicitly say that.

Either way, you will want to be more consistent than, say, the original beast in the 1933 version of *King Kong*, who tended to grow and shrink as necessary for the specific effects shot. But a quick look at a still of Kong atop the Empire State Building with a biplane in his hand gives us a rough idea of his size in that shot at least. One of the planes used in that movie was the Curtiss O2C-2, which had a wingspan of thirty-eight feet. That makes Kong about sixty feet tall. Usually it's better to compare than to specify—we don't specify, in general, when we're in a state of blind panic. Someone who's running for her life will tend to use less specific language: "It was huge!" or "That thing is as big as a house!"

But someone who is carefully observing the beast might be more descriptive. A more detached perspective on a creature's size is usually creepier as well, as we see in this excerpt from H.P. Lovecraft's story, "The Shadow Out of Time."

> The real horror began in May, 1915, when I first saw the living things. This was before my studies had taught me what, in view of the myths and case histories, to expect. As mental barriers wore down, I beheld great masses of thin vapour in various parts of the building and in the streets below.
>
> These steadily grew more solid and distinct, till at last I could trace their monstrous outlines with uncomfortable ease. They seemed to be enormous, iridescent cones, about ten feet high and ten feet wide at the base, and made up of some ridgy, scaly, semi-elastic matter. From their apexes projected four flexible, cylindrical members, each a foot thick, and of a ridgy substance like that of the cones themselves.
>
> These members were sometimes contracted almost to nothing, and sometimes extended to any distance up to about ten feet. Terminating two of them were enormous claws or nippers. At the end of a third were four red, trumpetlike appendages. The fourth terminated in an irregular yellowish globe some two feet in diameter and having three great dark eyes ranged along its central circumference.
>
> Surmounting this head were four slender grey stalks bearing flower-like appendages, whilst from its nether side dangled eight greenish antennae or tentacles. The great base of the central cone was fringed with a rubbery, grey substance which moved the whole entity through expansion and contraction.

Take note of the line that begins *As mental barriers wore down* ... We know that this character is beginning to observe this phenomenon from a more rational perspective, making the rather irrational nature of what he's describing all the more alien. It reveals something about the character who's experiencing the monster. We aren't wondering if maybe this is just a bear, for instance, and in his blind panic he perceives it to be Bigfoot.

Whatever the size of the thing, it's not at all a bad idea for you to know exactly how big it is and to have that information in your notes. That way you can avoid the growing and shrinking that King Kong undergoes. If you know exactly how heavy your monster is, with a little research you can figure out how something that heavy interacts with the environment around it. How much weight can the roof of a Brooklyn tenement building safely hold? Maybe twenty people, or around three thousand pounds? (Don't quote me on that!) If you want your monster to crash through the roof, make it heavier than three thousand pounds. If you want the roof to support your monster, make it lighter. And then, when a character who knows the building sees it crash through the roof, he can say, "That roof can hold up to three thousand pounds!" And now we know the monster is heavier than that without having to weigh it.

SMALL IS SCARY

In "Dreams in the Witch-House," Lovecraft cooked up this vicious little devil, which, unlike the creature in the previous Lovecraft example, is described not in specific measurements but in comparison to a more familiar animal.

> That object—no larger than a good-sized rat and quaintly called by the townspeople "Brown Jenkin"—seemed to have been the fruit of a remarkable case of sympathetic herd-delusion, for in 1692 no less than eleven persons had testified to glimpsing it. There were recent rumours, too, with a baffling and disconcerting amount of agreement. Witnesses said it had long hair and the shape of a rat, but that its sharp-toothed, bearded face was evilly human while its paws were like tiny human hands. It took messages betwixt old Keziah and the devil, and was nursed on the witch's blood, which it sucked like a vampire. Its voice was a kind of loathsome titter, and it could speak all languages. Of all the bizarre monstrosities in Gilman's dreams, nothing filled him with greater panic and

nausea than this blasphemous and diminutive hybrid, whose image flitted across his vision in a form a thousandfold more hateful than anything his waking mind had deduced from the ancient records and the modern whispers.

Between the "loathsome titter" and its human-rat features flitting across our vision, this little beast is not one we want to meet in an alley, much less feel scurrying up our leg in the dark.

Smaller yet, in *Hellboy II: The Golden Army*, we're treated to the tiny but terrifying tooth faeries. Although they're only a few inches tall, what makes them terrifying is that they eat your teeth first, so when they attack you get that fun bit of Novocain-free dentistry before they move on to devour the rest of you. And oh yeah, there are thousands of them.

And even on a microscopic level, the Ebola virus is described by Richard Preston in *The Hot Zone* as a little monster that's almost impossible to fight. You can't see a virus, let alone slash it with your trusty broadsword, shoot it with a blaster, or drive a stake through its heart. It gets inside you and starts eating, and the only reason you know it's there at all is the horrible effect it's having on your body.

Creepy!

Several of the top phobias listed in Chapter 2 reference various creepy crawlies that are far smaller than any human. Spiders and insects are tiny, but they scare us just the same. I've seen grown men freak out at the sight of a spider that is as small in comparison to us as we are to a skyscraper. Most of the time, I've seen that grown man in a bathroom mirror, but I won't tell if you don't. And we know on a rational level that bugs and spiders are animals, and that very few of them are in any way harmful to us, but we know that some are predators in their tiny worlds—gruesome predators. They're capable of killing and they're weird looking. That sounds a lot like our definition of a monster.

Yes, there's something entirely alien about insects and spiders, too. It's difficult, if not impossible, to look them in the eyes. An insect can't communicate what it's thinking—it really isn't even "thinking" in the way a mammal, let alone a human, thinks. We can't tell if it's more scared of us than we are of it—a common and invariably unsuccessful bit of parental wisdom I know we've all heard—or if it's using some kind of pheromone to signal the hive that it's found a tasty human, defenseless against the power of the swarm.

Small monsters, like Hellboy's tooth faeries, tend to travel in packs. This heightens the fear factor, because if you kill one, there are still dozens, hundreds, thousands, even millions more still nibbling away at you. One ant can't kill you, but a massive swarm of them might, as in Carl Stephenson's classic 1937 pulp adventure story "Leiningen versus the Ants":

> The Brazilian official threw up lean and lanky arms and clawed at the air with wildly distended fingers. "Leiningen!" he shouted. "You're insane! They're not creatures you can fight—they're an elemental—an 'act of God'! Ten miles long, two miles wide—ants, nothing but ants! And every single one of them a fiend from hell; before you can spit three times they'll eat a full-grown buffalo to the bones. I tell you if you don't clear out at once there'll be nothing left of you but a skeleton picked as clean as your own plantation."

This plays into the fear of thousands of small hurts—the death of a thousand bites.

So as you can see, enormous or microscopic, any size monster has the potential to frighten your readers in a big way.

CHAPTER 15

POWERS AND ABILITIES

What makes monsters inhuman and strange often comes in the form of what the old *Superman* TV series called "powers and abilities far beyond those of mortal men." In other words, this is where we answer the question: "What can this thing actually do?"

Taking another cue from the world of role-playing games, consider this handy list from the *Advanced Dungeons & Dragons Dungeon Master's Guide* by Gary Gygax,[1]

> Appendix D: Random Generation of Creatures from the Lower
> Planes
> SPECIAL ATTACKS
>   1. Ability drain
>   2. Energy drain (cold)
>   3. Gaseous discharge or missile discharge
>   4. Heat generation
>   5. Life level drain
>   6. Spell-like abilities
>   7. Spell use
>   8. Summon/gate

Before you pull out your eight-sided die (and for you nongamers out there, yes, there is such a thing as an eight-sided die!), randomly generating monsters wasn't necessarily even a good idea for the D&D Dungeon Master. But

---

1 *Advanced Dungeons & Dragons Dungeon Master's Guide* ©1979 TSR, Inc.

take a good look at these eight things that Gary Gygax came up with in 1979. Surely we can all add to this list with our own limitless imaginations. Things like "ability drain," "energy drain," and "life level drain" have specific game mechanics attached to them, but ultimately this means that the monster draws life energy from its victim, weakening him in some way. "Gaseous discharge" will be familiar to pug owners or Taco Bell customers—but what if that gas was a sort of naturally occurring nerve gas? "Missiles" can be quills, fireballs, or other things that allow the monster to strike from a distance. What else can we add? Can the monster heat up in a way that changes the environment around it or burns anything it touches? Is this monster coming from a world in which magic exists? That "spell-like ability" or "spell use" could make it a sort of natural wizard. And finally, "summon/gate" indicates that it can call forth others of its kind—or other, maybe even scarier monsters—from some distant locale or alternate dimension.

I'll repeat the warning that you do not necessarily *need* to create role-playing game (RPG) mechanics for your monsters or any other aspect of your worldbuilding before (or after) writing a screenplay, short story, or novel, but RPGs can still be fun and effective sources of inspiration, especially in terms of balancing out a monster's powers and weaknesses.

FROM THE MONSTER CREATION FORM: HOW SMART IS IT?

What can you compare your monster to in terms of its relative intelligence? Is it as smart as the average person, taking it into monster-as-villain territory? Is it as smart as the average wolf, making it a skilled and cunning hunter? Or is it entirely unintelligent, like some kind of giant amoeba? Answering this question on the form will suggest limits to its ability, too, and will have a significant effect on the form's next question: What motivates it?

In his story "The Shadow Out of Time," H.P. Lovecraft ran down some of the Elder Ones' inhuman traits.

According to these scraps of information, the basis of the fear was a horrible elder race of half-polypous, utterly alien entities which had come through space from immeasurably distant universes and had dominated the earth and three other solar planets about 600 million years ago. They were only partly material—as we understand matter—and their type of consciousness and media of perception differed widely from those of terrestrial organisms. For example, their senses did not include that of sight; their mental world being a strange, non-visual pattern of impressions.

They were, however, sufficiently material to use implements of normal matter when in cosmic areas containing it; and they required housing—albeit of a peculiar kind. Though their senses could penetrate all material barriers, their substance could not; and certain forms of electrical energy could wholly destroy them. They had the power of aerial motion, despite the absence of wings or any other visible means of levitation. Their minds were of such texture that no exchange with them could be effected by the Great Race.

If we render the powers of the Elder Ones in the form of a simple list, as Gary Gygax did, we'd get:

- Ability to travel through space
- Extrasensory perception that ignores solid barriers
- Partial incorporeality
- Ability to understand and use tools/technology
- Ability to fly
- Immunity to mind control

This is precisely the sort of list any monster maker should keep for all of his monstrous creations. Although this short list lacks the game mechanics necessary for use in a role-playing game, that's okay. Those mechanics are unnecessary for pure storytelling. Still, your own notes should be even more descriptive than those above. Keep in mind that comparing the monster's relative power to human traits or the traits of other animals can help in balancing things.

So what if we took the mechanics out of the description of *Primeval Thule*'s Star-thing of Nheb, which we examined earlier, and described it not for the game, but for a story:

- A star-thing can shift from the Material Plane to the Ethereal Plane, and sometimes it can take another creature with it. A star-thing can only remain ethereal for about five minutes and then must return to the Material Plane. It cannot use this ability again for twice as long as it was shifted into the Ethereal plane.
- A star-thing's tentacles slowly drain the life force from a victim, sapping the victim's basic health and fortitude.
- A star-thing is able to conjure strange lights that have a hypnotic effect on its victims.
- A star-thing is twice as strong as the average man and able to both swim and climb with ease.
- A star-thing is able to teleport once a day—it disappears in a flash and instantly reappears at any distant location known to it.
- Three times a day a star-thing can appear to blur, making it harder to pinpoint its location; it can cause a victim to stay anchored to an alternate dimension, unable to return to its home plane of existence, and it's able to dispel the magical effects of another's spells, enchanted items, etc.

That's a pretty long and involved list that adds up to a sort of basic modus operandi: The star-thing mesmerizes its intended victim to make it easier to grab up in its life-draining tentacles, then it absconds with that poor soul into an alternate dimension, traps him there, and goes back for more. It collects these victims in a sort of larder, feeding off their very life essences in its own horrifyingly alien way.

The reason that some of the star-thing's abilities only work once or three times a day is largely one of game balance, or in the case of your monster, story balance. The limits to a monster's powers are not the same as weaknesses but are simply caps on the being's otherworldly might. You have to give your hero an opportunity to defeat this beast, right? So before applying that sort of limit, think about the reason for it and how those limitations can become opportunities for your hero and serve the greater story.

Can a dragon breathe fire with every breath? Or does it have to recharge in some way? Does it have to eat something to recharge? Dragons aren't real, so I don't know the answer to those questions. The answer can be anything you like—anything that serves your story—but remember, consistency is king, so if that dragon discharges a torrent of fire eight breaths in a row in Chapter Six then can barely manage two in Chapter Twenty, what's changed?

Likewise if the monster is "really strong," how strong is "really" strong? If it's "really smart," how smart is "really" smart? You don't have to be exact, but you should be descriptive and clear about these traits, if only for yourself. Is it so intelligent that it qualifies as a villain (or hero) instead? Or if it can fly, how high and how fast can it fly, and does it have limitations? H.P. Lovecraft determined a sort of limit to a monster's ability to fly in "The Whisperer in Darkness."

> The things come from another planet, being able to live in interstellar space and fly through it on clumsy, powerful wings which have a way of resisting the aether but which are too poor at steering to be of much use in helping them about on earth.

The creatures can fly well enough in space, it seems, using their powerful yet clumsy wings, but they are less adept at flying in Earth's atmosphere. Again, this is an example of a limitation more than a weakness.

And in the previous example from Lovecraft's "The Shadow Out of Time," we learn something of the limits of the monster's senses. Lovecraft states that "their senses did not include that of sight; their mental world being a strange, non-visual pattern of impressions." Can your monster see in the dark? Can it smell blood like a shark? Limiting a monster's senses can give your characters a chance for survival, but apply those limitations carefully and balance them with other abilities. Consider the Tyrannosaur in *Jurassic Park*. It can't see its victims if they don't move, but can it smell them? Can it hear them? Your monster may possess some, none, or all of the five senses and/or some other sense entirely. Some animals like bats and whales have natural sonar. A shark's lateral line can detect electrical impulses in the water. It's hard for us to imagine what that might feel like, but no one ever said writing a monster story was going to be easy!

Back to the star-thing for a moment: Notice that some of its special abilities take certain physical forms, most notably the tentacles with their life-draining properties. These could just as easily have been life-draining hands, fangs, or all sorts of other limbs or protuberances.

Looking to the animal kingdom for inspirational physical traits is always a good idea, as animals tend to be very specialized in appearance based on how and what they eat. Horses don't need hands to graze, but they do need long necks to help them dip their mouths to the ground and flat teeth to grind vegetable matter. Tentacles are good for holding onto something long enough to kill or paralyze it, as any squid or snake—whose body is essentially one big tentacle—could tell you.

Marrying the physical form of the creature with its powers and abilities lends them an additional level of verisimilitude, or what we've been calling "plausibility."

Then again, not all monsters need to be grounded in reality—in fact, some of the most effective monsters are frightening because they're so alien to anything we've experienced in the animal kingdom. In his story "At the Mountains of Madness," H.P. Lovecraft described the horrible Shoggoths using very few real, animalistic traits.

> They had always been controlled through the hypnotic suggestions of the Old Ones, and had modeled their tough plas-

ticity into various useful temporary limbs and organs; but now their self-modeling powers were sometimes exercised independently, and in various imitative forms implanted by past suggestion. They had, it seems, developed a semistable brain whose separate and occasionally stubborn volition echoed the will of the Old Ones without always obeying it. Sculptured images of these Shoggoths filled Danforth and me with horror and loathing. They were normally shapeless entities composed of a viscous jelly which looked like an agglutination of bubbles, and each averaged about fifteen feet in diameter when a sphere. They had, however, a constantly shifting shape and volume—throwing out temporary developments or forming apparent organs of sight, hearing, and speech in imitation of their masters, either spontaneously or according to suggestion.

This is a monster that can be anything and ends up being, more or less, a blob. But Lovecraft loved the idea of a monster you can't comprehend, let alone fight. Even worse, a monster whose mere existence will drive you insane, so the only thing you can hope for is that it will not notice you, and you'll be able to live out your life gibbering away in a padded room somewhere.

Sometimes just being itself is all the "power" a monster needs.

CHAPTER 16

WEAKNESSES

> After weeks of throwing everything they had at it, from nuclear weapons to promises of appeasement, from 'Please Don't Destroy Us All' cards to the most toxic nerve gas ever imagined by human science, the last human on Earth was eaten alive by the great, raging Zuglath. The monster chewed, swallowed, burped, then laid down for a nap.

So ends a story of a monster with no weaknesses.

Kind of a tough story to pull off, and one not everybody's going to love. That doesn't mean you can't give it a try, but the rest of this chapter is for those authors who'd like to give their heroes a fighting chance.

As Thieves' World series co-creator Lynn Abbey says, "Unless the writer intends for the monster to be the 'last man standing' after the climax, it's going to need a weakness and the characters are going to have to exploit it."

In other words, what makes it possible to kill or otherwise dispose of this thing?

Remember, a monster's limitations are the furthest extents of its powers, but a weakness is something that can allow your characters to hurt or kill it. For example, your vampires might have all the abilities of a nocturnal creature as well as superhuman strength and hypnosis, but it must sleep during the day and it can't enter your home without an invitation. These are limitations that your characters can exploit. You can physically hurt or even kill your vampire by playing against its weaknesses. By now we all have a pretty good idea of a vampire's weaknesses:

- Garlic
- Crucifixes
- A wooden stake through the heart
- Setting it on fire
- Drowning
- Beheading
- Sunlight (usually ... oddly enough, Bram Stoker's famed vampire could operate during the day from time to time, although his powers were greatly weakened)

It's interesting to note that over the years authors have taken some of these weaknesses away and have come up with new ones, or as Lynn Abbey advises: "If the monster in question is of a known species or archetypical creature, and its weaknesses are likewise apparent, then the writer's job is to tweak the tropes—is this particular vampire really sensitive to light? To all light, or just sunlight?"

THE MONSTER CREATION FORM: WHAT HURTS IT?

This whole chapter is dedicated to that single entry on our monster form, so look to the text for prompts. But for purposes of the form, which is meant to be a simple, top-down distillation of your monster, think about the *unusual* weakness, the *unexpected* weakness ... It's come to invade Earth, which is essentially a water planet—but it's burned by water. Or, the only way to kill it is by forcing it to look into its own soul. That's a tough one, but it sounds like a story worth reading!

What we've come to accept as the archetypical zombie is a fascinating example of how one movie, *Night of the Living Dead* by George A. Romero, gave birth to a mythology that's progressed far beyond that single film—and far beyond Romero's own continuing franchise, too. Though there's an ongoing argument between fans of Romero's slow, shuffling zombies and the so-called "fast zombies" of the remakes, most zombie stories tend to agree that you have to destroy a zombie's brain in order to destroy the zombie. Different explanations exist for why/how the brain, or something inside the brain, allows a zombie to move and get around. This is its weakness, whereas its slow speed and abysmally low physical dexterity are limitations. Watching the zombie mythology develop over the years has been fascinating, and one can only imagine what it's like to be in the writer's room for AMC's *The Walking Dead* as they come up with all the ways you can destroy someone's brain.

In order to break new ground with old tropes, authors of horror, fantasy, and science fiction often need to go to some of the darkest corners of our imagination. And the creators of the video game *Dead Space* went into very dark places indeed with the creation of the necromorphs: zombie-inspired undead creatures that can be killed only by total dismemberment. You can't just shoot a necromorph in the head, you have to literally chop it into pieces. It's the fact that they're so hard to kill that makes them truly alien. This is a monster that doesn't die the way everything else in the real world dies, and as the hero of the game, you have to figure out how to overcome this particularly difficult "weakness."

Lynn Abbey has the same ideas in terms of forcing characters to explore a monster's strengths and weaknesses in order to defeat it, in the same way it's not always obvious in *Dead Space* just what you should be shooting at. She asserts that "the characters' triumph will be most satisfying if the writer has portrayed them as far more intelligent and resourceful than lucky."

But how to do that?

"To pull this off, the writer needs to know both the monster's flaw and how the characters will exploit it from the get-go," Abbey says. "I'd go as far as to say that you plot a monster story in reverse: Start with the monster's fall, then dismantle the characters' knowledge and preparation, then construct the plot details that allow the characters to pick up the pieces they're going to need."

Going back to the important idea of plausibility, think through the monster's weaknesses as carefully as you do its powers, description, and so on—maybe even more so, since its weaknesses are directly related to the heart of your story's resolution (or at least the resolution of the part of your story in which the monster appears).

The aliens in the movie *Signs*, for instance, have a weakness that stretches plausibility: They're burned by water. So why would these creatures, who are smart enough to travel faster than the speed of light in starships big enough to transport whole armies using a cloaking device, choose to invade a world that's more than 70 percent water—and do so, apparently, naked?

And who says a monster's weakness has to be a physical thing? Does it have to come down to *How do we kill it*? Instead of having your characters wonder whether they should cut its head off or shoot it, maybe your story compels them to figure out how to understand the monster, befriend it, or give it what it wants. Communication might be a challenge with your monster, and overcoming that challenge might turn your monster into a sympathetic antagonist, or at least become less threatening.

Also think about weaknesses in terms of how this might make the monster identifiable. The monster may be among us, unrecognizable except for one little giveaway—its weakness. "Most folkloric monsters have something that not only lessens their advantage over ordinary people, it alerts regular people to the danger in their midst," Chelsea Quinn Yarbro, author of the Saint-Germain Cycle, says. "For example, in Eastern Europe, witches were thought to have no shadows, so if an old woman lacked a shadow it was proof positive she was a witch. Monsters in folklore often display inappropriate behavior that once again gives ordinary people a signal that something is amiss."

In "Beyond the Wall of Sleep," Lovecraft merges the weakness of a human victim with the cosmic entity that possesses him, making the human body itself the monster's primary weakness.

"Joe Slater is dead," came the soul-petrifying voice of an agency from beyond the wall of sleep. My opened eyes sought the couch of pain in curious horror, but the blue eyes were still calmly gazing, and the countenance was still intelligently animated. "He is better dead, for he was unfit to bear the active intellect of cosmic entity. His gross body could not undergo the needed adjustments between ethereal life and planet life. He was too much an animal, too little a man; yet it is through his deficiency that you have come to discover me, for the cosmic and planet souls rightly should never meet. He has been my torment and diurnal prison for forty-two of your terrestrial years."

Monsters that can hide in plain sight by taking on human form or the form of some animal or inanimate object might still give off some kind of smell, as in Algernon Blackwood's "The Wendigo." Or maybe the monster in disguise seems otherworldly somehow, almost unnatural compared to the people around him, as is the case with the young boy in Lovecraft's classic "The Dunwich Horror."

His speech was somewhat remarkable both because of its difference from the ordinary accents of the region, and because it displayed a freedom from infantile lisping of which many children of three or four might well be proud. The boy was not talkative, yet when he spoke he seemed to reflect some elusive element wholly unpossessed by Dunwich and its denizens. The strangeness did not reside in what he said, or even in the simple idioms he used; but seemed vaguely linked with his intonation or with the internal organs that produced the spoken sounds. His facial aspect, too, was remarkable for its maturity; for though he shared his mother's and grandfather's chinlessness, his firm and precociously shaped nose united with the expression of his large, dark, almost Latin eyes to give him an air of quasi-adulthood and well-nigh preternatural intelligence. He was, however, exceedingly ugly despite his appearance of brilliancy; there being something almost goatish or animalistic about his thick lips, large-pored, yellowish skin, coarse crinkly hair, and oddly elongated ears. He was soon disliked even more decidedly than his mother and grandsire, and all conjectures about him were spiced with references to the bygone magic of Old Whateley, and how the hills once shook when he shrieked the dreadful name of *Yog-Sothoth* in the midst of a circle of stones with a great book open in his arms before him. Dogs abhorred the boy, and he was always obliged to take various defensive measures against their barking menace.

Whatever evil resides within this boy, it is not wholly secret as the dogs know something is inherently wrong, and even other citizens notice something "animalistic" about him. The town is turning against this boy, but they don't know why ... it's instinct. And a monster cannot control that. The potential for this sort of ephemeral, nonphysical weakness is absolutely infinite—your imagination is the only limit.

Keep in mind that what's good for the monster is good for the hero. Or, as author Brendan Deneen puts it, "I think every character, hero or villain, angel or monster, needs a weakness, a vulnerability. The more subtle the weakness, the stronger the character. A monster with a subtle emotional/psychological weakness? That is super interesting in my book."

Speaking of an emotional weakness, who doesn't remember the classic last line from *King Kong*: "It was beauty killed the beast." Was Kong possessive of Anne Darrow? Was he protecting her from what he saw as threats (the ship's crew on the island, the police and airplanes in New York)? Or was he just saving her for a tasty midnight snack? Whatever the motivation, it was Kong's single-minded attraction to a beautiful blonde that was his tragic downfall.

That makes Kong the ultimate everyman.

CHAPTER 17

DESCRIPTION

Just as a shark would seem to be a monster if you've never experienced one before, the same would be true for a tiger. If you'd never heard of tigers, never saw a picture of one, and then walked around a corner into an alley and ran into a full-grown Bengal tiger, it would stop you in your tracks. What sort of a creature is this? From the teeth, the claws, the musculature, and the piercing eyes, you might decide that it's a dangerous predator. Humans, like any other animal, experience a primitive fight-or-flight response when faced with a danger such as this. We can recognize a predator. We may even sense how it sees us and anticipate its intentions. Our reaction is part instinct, part observation.

But a tiger is also physically beautiful. When we see tigers on TV or at the zoo, we can admire their subtle grace and the color and patterns of their coats. We can watch them interact with their cubs and begin to see the similarities they have with domesticated cats. And we can collect information about their behavior. A tiger that purrs is less scary than a tiger that roars.

This begs the question: Does a monster have to be ugly?

The fast answer is, no, of course not. In fact, your monsters can look as beautiful or as ugly, as alien or as familiar, as you wish. A pretty songbird might seem harmless in real life, but place it in the hands of Alfred Hitchcock and it might become part of a killer swarm.

Consider this brief excerpt from *The Coldest Girl in Coldtown* by Holly Black.

> Even from the beginning, that was the problem. People liked
> pretty things. People even liked pretty things that wanted to
> kill and eat them.

"Pretty" monsters are still deadly ones, and they are as old as Homer's sirens, as tempting as Dracula's "brides," and as nouveau as the inhuman robot women of Ira Levin's *The Stepford Wives*.

Monsters can be pretty, and monsters can be pretty ugly. Slimy monsters are scarier to children's book author and editor Nina Hess: "Hairy monsters feel like they could be potentially friendly or at least are merchandised as quirky, cute stuffed animals."

Unless that quirky, furry Bengal tiger takes a bite out of you!

Beyond simple choices like *pretty, slimy, hairy*, and *ugly*, word choice is just as important in the description of a monster as it is in any part of your writing, even if your monster is almost impossible to describe, as in this line from Lovecraft's "The Unnamable."

> It was everywhere—a gelatin—a slime yet it had shapes, a
> thousand shapes of horror beyond all memory. There were
> eyes—and a blemish. It was the pit—the maelstrom—the ul-
> timate abomination.

Sometimes even the masters will assert that there's simply no single word or phrase in the English language that will tell you exactly what this thing looks like, and working that undescribable assertion into the description suffices. It may feel like a cheat to dance around an exact or simple description, so use this technique sparingly and carefully.

THE MONSTER CREATION FORM: WHAT DOES IT LOOK LIKE?

The monster form prompts you to list common features, but this by no means should be taken as either a complete list or as a mandate. Your monster does not have to have a nose at all, for instance. There are blind cavefish that have no eyes—not functional eyes, anyway. So if your monster comes from a place of complete darkness, after the "Eyes" entry you may want to simply state, "none."

Look to the text in Chapter 14, "Size," to help you fill in that line and think about ways to compare it to known objects: It's a Neanderthal as tall as a three-story building, or it's a lizard the size of a railroad car, or it's a robot no bigger than the common cold virus.

This is also where you can brainstorm about what covers its body, answering the age-old question "Furry or slimy?" once and for all. And as for the color of the thing, here's an opportunity to pause and ask yourself, "Why?" There are a lot of green insects and reptiles in the jungle because that coloring helps these creatures blend into the surrounding foliage—it's camouflage. So if your monster is bright blue, *why*? How does that help your monster survive in its natural environment—if it has a "natural" environment at all?

SHOW VS. TELL

Surely the most common words of advice given to any fiction author are "show, don't tell." But what does that mean, exactly?

In prose fiction, as opposed to visual media like movies and video games, you have to get much deeper into a monster's physical description whether or not the physical description aligns with or plays against the creature's true intent. What comes effortlessly in a movie requires vividly written description in prose.

Obviously you can't just say, "The monster jumped out, and it was scary." You can't just tell readers it's scary, you have show how scary it is using carefully chosen words and effective descriptions. You have to explore that dark territory with all of your senses, otherwise your writing is not going to be effective.

Allow—even force—your readers to join in the visceral experience of that monster. At some point you will need to describe what it looks like, but what's most interesting, most compelling, and most terrifying, is what the monster actually does and the effect that it has on the people who encounter it.

For example, if you tell your reader, "Arron fought off the monster," your writing will just lay there like a lump on a log. Instead describe the sensations of the moment—negative or positive. This example is from a novella, *The Haunting of Dragon's Cliff*, that I co-wrote with Mel Odom.

> The creature's hand came down on his left shoulder and squeezed his studded leather shoulder harness into his flesh. The collarbone beneath it bent, and was about to break, so Arron kicked up hard between the thing's legs. He could feel, even through his heavy boot, that he'd hit his mark. But the Stablehand's reaction was hardly what Arron expected. He was sure the great brute, big and strong as he was, would react the way any man would to a blow like that—and Arron had kicked him hard—but instead of a squeal or even a groan, the giant only sighed. Instead of falling to his knees, he lifted Arron up off the ground by his shoulder. Instead of a look of agonizing pain, the Stablehand appeared only sad, defeated, his features sagging and his white eyes blank.
>
> Arron punched him in the face. The barbarian felt something give—a broken cheekbone—but the Stablehand didn't flinch. Instead, the monster wrapped him up with his free hand around his back and pressed him into his barrel chest. The flesh stank, and was slick with putrid slime. Arron tried to pull back and managed at least to keep from getting any of it in his mouth.

Another visceral example that has strong physical cues is found in Anne McCaffrey's fantasy classic *Dragonflight*.[1]

> Quickly she thudded down the stairs, crossing to the watch-wher. It cried piteously, its great eyes blinking against the growing daylight. Oblivious to the stench of its rank breath, she hugged the scaly head to her, scratching its ears and eye ridges. The watch-wher was ecstatic with pleasure, its long body trembling, its

---

[1] Del Rey 1968, ©1968 Anne McCaffrey

clipped wings rustling. It alone knew who she was or cared. And it was the only creature in all Pern she had trusted since the dawn she had blindly sought refuge in its dark, stinking lair to escape the thirsty swords that had drunk so deeply of Ruathan blood.

McCaffrey's description of the watch-wher stresses the point-of-view character's emotional reaction and attachment to the monster, her memory, her senses, and her experience of the place and time described in the novel. The watch-wher cries "piteously," which is clearly this character's interpretation of that sound. Its eyes are described in the context of the time of day, also telling us that maybe they're sensitive to bright light. The fact that she's "oblivious to the stench of its rank breath" tells us two things: She likes this creature enough to ignore its shortcomings, and it has bad breath. We only know it's scaly because she touches it—hugs it, actually. How do we know it has eye ridges? Because she scratches them. As she describes what's happening, she's anthropomorphizing the monster, reacting to it as if it were a pet as we learn more about its physical form: It has a long body and clipped wings. Then the author further defines the relationship between character and monster, making it clear that a special connection exists between them—and a traumatic history.

But most of all, from the character's reaction to the watch-wher we know that this is not a monster to be afraid of, at least not in this instance.

Now look at what a single word can do to convey the frightening nature of an unknown monster.

This I ask myself, but ever does there come before me a hideously vivid vision in reply. I cannot think of the deep sea without shuddering at the nameless things that may at this very moment be crawling and floundering on its slimy bed, worshipping their ancient stone idols and carving their own detestable likenesses on the submarine obelisks of water-soaked granite.

This is from the short story "Dagon" by H.P. Lovecraft, and the single word is *shuddering*. This describes the character's physical reaction to the unknown monsters of the deep. Now consider this rewrite.

> This I ask myself, but ever does there come before me a hideous-
> ly vivid vision in reply. I cannot think of the deep sea without
> being afraid of the nameless things that may at this very mo-
> ment be crawling and floundering on its slimy bed, worship-
> ping their ancient stone idols and carving their own detestable
> likenesses on the submarine obelisks of water-soaked granite.

All I did was replace "shuddering at" with "being afraid of," but doesn't the latter example feel more detached, more at a distance, despite every other word being the same?

And often it's just as effective to describe what's so frightening about a monster as it is to describe the aftermath of the monster. What if you walk into a room and the floor is covered in bones and there are webs all over the ceiling and you're thinking, *Something is in here. This is not good.* You're seeing that the monster has done something terrible, but where is it? It might still be in here!

In the pilot episode of *The Walking Dead*, after Rick wakes up in the hospital, quite a long time goes by before we actually encounter our first zombie. Rick has to walk a gauntlet of blood-spattered walls, mutilated corpses, abandoned military posts, crashed cars, and empty streets. He has no idea what's gone on while he lay in a coma, but whatever it was, it was bad and it was big.

POINT OF VIEW

You should always write from a very strict point of view (POV), whether in first or third person. I feel that first- or third-person-limited viewpoint makes your writing more effective because ultimately what we're reading isn't just the story of a person, but everything being filtered through that person's emotions, history, experience, preconceptions, and so on. It always feels more personal.

So in a monster story, when we experience a person experiencing this monster, processing the monster through that filter, it brings the narrative to life for the reader. What does the character think and feel?

Is he scared? Angry? What is the visceral, emotional reaction that this person is having to this situation right now?

And one of the more important questions: What does the POV character know?

By the time they go out in the boat, the police chief, the marine biologist, and the shark fisherman in *Jaws* know that they're going to hunt a really big man-eating shark. On the other hand, the girl in the very beginning of the story has no idea that monster fish is out there. She's just enjoying a beach party, decides to take a quick skinny dip, and all of a sudden—*boom*—this unseen thing just hits her from under the water.

By the time the fishing expedition sets out, the characters have caught up with what the readers know, and the story of *Jaws* has hit a common tipping point in monster stories. It becomes more of an adventure story—in this case quite overtly in the tradition of *Moby Dick*—than a horror story. The characters know what they're up against, and they're off to fight it.

Apex predators that we are, we tend to be goal oriented or object oriented when it comes to other animals, so when we're presented with a specific creature to fight, it's not necessarily as panic-inducing as trying to figure out what's eating everyone. Now your character says, "Well, I have this problem with a shark that I have to solve. I better gather X, Y, and Z and go fix this." It can still be a scary situation—the shark in *Jaws* didn't suddenly become a lake trout once they knew what they were hunting. Instead of the fear of the unknown, fear in this situation comes from a sense of urgency, of the choices we need to make in a miniscule amount of time, and of the full knowledge of the terrible consequences of getting something wrong. The reader is right there with the characters as they start to think rapidly, *Can I swim away, can I fight it, can I do this or that or the other thing?*

But say something's making noise out there in the dark, and the POV character doesn't know what it is. It could be a squirrel, and you're not afraid of squirrels. But it could also be some Lovecraftian horror from the center of the galaxy, and you better damn well be afraid of that.

Lots of monster stories have capitalized on the fear of the unknown by keeping a strict eye on POV and what the reader is shown throughout the story. Whether you intentionally restrict the characters' ability to understand or see the monster, or you are forced to do so (as was the case in the movie *Jaws*: the mechanical shark wasn't working properly, so the filmmakers had to shoot around it), it has become a well-known and effective truism in writing horror that what you don't show is often more frightening than what you describe in detail.

The Blair Witch Project is one of the scariest movies of all time because the monster is always something somewhere "out there," and we the audience only see and hear what the three characters see and hear because we're out there, lost with them. We don't see the monster; we just see the clues that it's nearby—as well as the effect it has on the characters.

At one point in that movie, one of the characters disappears and the next morning the others find some sort of little shrine that's been put together by some unknown agency in the middle of the night— disturbingly close to their tent. They investigate and find a piece of cloth from the missing character's shirt, which they open to reveal a handful of bloody human teeth.

For my money, that's much more effective than showing a separate scene of a monster-dentist at work. We all know how much it would hurt to have our teeth pulled out, and we're left to imagine the mechanism by which that was accomplished. This strong young man was overpowered, restrained, his jaws pried open ... and whatever could do that is still out there, circling us in the dark.

This is all about point of view. *The Blair Witch Project* was largely shot in close-up with unstable handheld cameras, so we see the terror in the characters' eyes and hear it in their voices, and while we're right there with them, we sometimes can't see even what the characters are seeing. It's possible to write prose "in close-up" as well, by concentrating on the minute detail of that quivering lip, tear-filled eye, the breathless quality of a gasp ... and letting your reader's imaginations run away with them.

CHAPTER 18

THE FIVE SENSES

We experience the world around us through a combination of our five senses: sight, hearing, scent, touch, and taste. Your writing should always appeal to as many of those senses as possible in an effort to make the experience more human. Having said that, eliminating one of those senses, or all but one, can help to accentuate a feeling of dread, helplessness, and loss of control, and really help you "write scary."

Director Peter Jackson's remake of *King Kong* contains an outstandingly effective example of how an audience's experience can be manipulated by simply taking one of the senses away or muting it. Movies often barrage us with sound, but in the scene in *King Kong* in the giant bug-infested trench, the music stops, there's very little dialogue, and the sounds we can hear are the subtle and deeply unsettling sounds of the monsters themselves. From that scene we learn a valuable lesson: When your characters are most in danger, take away all distractions.

When we're really in danger we tend to get a sort of tunnel vision—and our other senses "tunnel in" as well. In a normal conversation happening in a safe place, part of your mind is thinking, *Did I remember to mail my car payment*? Or, *I could really go for a hot dog right now*. But if you're being attacked by a giant scorpion, all that's on your mind is the giant scorpion—that's all. It has your full attention, and all five senses are tuned in only to that.

Consider the following sense aspects of your monster.

WHAT DOES IT LOOK LIKE?

The physical description of the beast is the most obvious starting point for the writer but not necessarily the best for the reader.

"We're very visual creatures," says author Richard Baker, "and seeing something allows us to precisely define what we're up against. We might not like what we discover, but it's no longer a mystery. This is why moviemakers are careful not to let you see the whole monster until the very end of the film—once that uncertainty is dispelled, you lose that element of self-inflicted dread and foreboding the reader or viewer is providing for you."

In the next chapter we'll discuss revealing monsters in stages, but once the time is right to reveal what this monster looks like, you'll want to bring to bear all your powers of description. Consider this description of the Deep Ones from H.P. Lovecraft's "The Shadow Over Innsmouth."

> I think their predominant colour was a greyish-green, though they had white bellies. They were mostly shiny and slippery, but the ridges of their backs were scaly. Their forms vaguely suggested the anthropoid, while their heads were the heads of fish, with prodigious bulging eyes that never closed. At the sides of their necks were palpitating gills, and their long paws were webbed. They hopped irregularly, sometimes on two legs and sometimes on four. I was somehow glad that they had no more than four limbs.

This comes across like a list of features, closed out by what seems a half-serious personal observation. But the real question is: What does this description tell us about the POV character?

Some people are able to experience even really weird things from a clinical perspective, as we see in the example, but that doesn't necessarily make what they're observing any less dangerous. And when the thing being described is obviously alien and dangerous, that psychological distance is filled in with your reader's own imagination, the unsettling thought of what it might feel like to be grabbed by one of those long, webbed paws.

In *A Wizard of Earthsea*,[1] author Ursula K. Le Guin dramatically narrowed that perceived distance between character and monster to create a sensation of immediate danger,

> And through that bright misshapen breach clambered something like a clot of black shadow, quick and hideous, and it leaped as if to attack.

That's much more about what the monster is doing (leaping to attack) and how fast it's doing it (quick) than what it looks like. Later in the same scene:

> Ged fell, struggling and writhing, while the bright rip in the world's darkness above him widened and stretched. The boys that watched fled, and Jasper bent down to the ground hiding his eyes from the terrible light. Vetch alone ran forward to his friend. So only he saw the lump of shadow that clung to Ged, tearing at his flesh. It was like a black beast, the size of a young child, though it seemed to swell and shrink; and it had no head or face, only the four taloned paws with which it gripped and tore.

Now panic has set in and what we're experiencing is the POV character's experience of what the other people in the scene are doing—their reaction to the monster and the "rip" it has come through. Still, the monster itself is simply a "lump of shadow." Once it stops tearing at his flesh with its talons, maybe Ged will have a chance to get a closer look.

Lynn Abbey said, "If I were a character confronting the monster, I'd definitely opt for sight. We're sight hunters; we're at our best extracting information with our eyes. So, as the writer, if I wanted to make things easiest for my characters, I'd give them visual information ... but I'm not

---

1 Houghton Mifflin 2012, ©1968 Ursula K. LeGuin

usually that kind to my characters. I'd probably leave them in the dark and make them think with their ears."

Bringing us to ...

WHAT DOES IT SOUND LIKE?

When we can't see for whatever reason—it's too dark, we're in murky water, there's some object blocking our line of sight—we have a tendency to fall back on our hearing.

Two video games in particular make tremendous use of the digital surround sound tools available to them. In both *BioShock* and *Dead Space* there's an almost constant barrage of sound effects: ambient sounds punctuated by echoing screams or bursts of frenzied, faraway dialogue that sometimes herald the appearance of an enemy but often exist simply to keep the player spooked. And if you've played either of these games, you know how well that works.

We're all hardwired to pay attention to certain sense cues. "Think about taking the trash out to the curb on a dark night and all of a sudden you hear a rattle, a thump, or a hiss without seeing anything," Richard Baker suggests. "That stops you in your tracks!"

When someone screams, that gets our attention. When we know there might be predators around and we hear a bang—or worse, the scrape of claws on the floor tile—that gets our attention, too. But if there's a lot of background noise, it's more difficult to pick the single significant note out of the mass of sounds. The two games mentioned above make use of that unsettling sense of mystery.

In the sword-and-sorcery classic *Red Nails*, Robert E. Howard introduces the presence of a monster by having his characters hear it first.

> "The horses should be beyond that thicket, over there," whispered Conan, and his voice might have been a breeze moving through the branches. "Listen!"

Valeria had already heard, and a chill crept through her veins; so she unconsciously laid her white hand on her companion's muscular brown arm. From beyond the thicket came the noisy crunching of bones and the loud rending of flesh, together with the grinding, slobbering sounds of a horrible feast.

"Lions wouldn't make that noise," whispered Conan. "Something's eating our horses, but it's not a lion—Crom!"

We know what an eyewitness is, but how often do we actually hear the testimony of, for lack of a better term, an ear-witness? Here's an example from Lovecraft's masterpiece, "The Dunwich Horror."

"It must be allow'd, that these Blasphemies of an infernall Train of Daemons are Matters of too common Knowledge to be deny'd; the cursed Voices of Azazel and Buzrael, of Beelzebub and Belial, being heard now from under Ground by above a Score of credible Witnesses now living. I myself did not more than a Fortnight ago catch a very plain Discourse of evill Powers in the Hill behind my House; wherein there were a Rattling and Rolling, Groaning, Screeching, and Hissing, such as no Things of this Earth could raise up, and which must needs have come from those Caves that only black Magick can discover, and only the Divell unlock."

Above we see a character reacting exclusively to sound. And in "The Unnamable," Lovecraft first introduces us to the unnamed monster through sound.

I heard a creaking sound through the pitchy blackness, and knew that a lattice window was opening in that accursed old house beside us. And because all the other frames were long since fallen, I knew that it was the grisly glassless frame of that demoniac attic window.

And then in the next paragraph, Lovecraft focuses on yet another sense ...

WHAT DOES IT SMELL LIKE?

Then came a noxious rush of noisome, frigid air from that same dreaded direction...

Let's all get together right now and work to bring back the word *noisome*!

How many times has a friend of yours smelled something terrible, made that screwed-up face, maybe even said, "Ugh, that's awful," then held it out to you and said, "Here ... smell this"?

And you've actually smelled it?

It's hard to resist smelling something bad, but once we do it, we instantly regret it. Things that smell bad are often poisonous or diseased, like rotten meat, and the bad smell is warning us away. But in some cases, that terrible smell is a defensive response. Some plant and animal species use foul odors to protect themselves from predators. But at the same time, both plants and animals use pheromones as a reproductive tool—or even to attract prey.

When thinking about what your monster smells like, consider why it might smell bad or why it might be better if it smells good. Does this thing use scent to mark its territory or mark its prey to make it easier to track down? Or, like a skunk, does it produce a bad smell to drive would-be predators away?

When it's raining, or has just rained, my dog smells funny when he comes in from outside. We say he smells like worms or mud. So be sure to consider how the smell of your monster changes depending on its environment. Astronauts have reported a distinct smell to moon dust—what does your alien planet smell like, and if your alien monster is covered in dirt from that place, does it carry the distinctive smell of gunpowder (like the Apollo astronauts reported) or onions or decayed vegetation or ... anything?

WHAT DOES IT FEEL LIKE?

This paragraph from H.P. Lovecraft's "The Dream-Quest of Unknown Kadath" has a character fleeing from a monster in complete darkness, trying to rely on hearing to warn him of the creature's approach, but it's the sense of touch that's most terrifying.

> Sound travels slowly, so it was some time before he heard an answering glibber. But it came at last, and before long he was told that a rope ladder would be lowered. The wait for this was very tense, since there was no telling what might not have been stirred up among those bones by his shouting. Indeed, it was not long before he actually did hear a vague rustling afar off. As this thoughtfully approached, he became more and more uncomfortable; for he did not wish to move away from the spot where the ladder would come. Finally the tension grew almost unbearable, and he was about to flee in panic when the thud of something on the newly heaped bones nearby drew his notice from the other sound. It was the ladder, and after a minute of groping he had it taut in his hands. But the other sound did not cease, and followed him even as he climbed. He had gone fully five feet from the ground when the rattling beneath waxed emphatic, and was a good ten feet up when something swayed the ladder from below. At a height which must have been fifteen or twenty feet he felt his whole side brushed by a great slippery length which grew alternately convex and concave with wriggling; and hereafter he climbed desperately to escape the unendurable nuzzling of that loathsome and overfed Dhole whose form no man might see.

The "nuzzling" is a nice touch, as many real animals will test something before eating it (sharks bump their victims, for example). But it also gives the sense that this giant thing may be blind, too, searching for its prey, and you came *that* close to becoming a chew toy.

It's important to remember that what a monster looks like, smells like, and feels like are often very closely interrelated. If your monster is slimy, like a slug, for instance, it will appear shiny, you might be able to hear it slithering along, and the trail of slime might have some distinctive smell. All of those cues tend to add up for most people as a warning not to touch the slimy thing. You don't want to get any of that on you.

If the monster is hairy or furry, that's only a start. What does that fur feel like: Is it coarse and wiry or soft? Is your fantasy barbarian tempted to make a coat out of its fur or use it to sharpen his sword?

Most fish feel very smooth, but a shark's skin is like sandpaper.

A look at the animal kingdom reveals a huge range of diversity from creatures with cold, hard shells like crabs to things that hardly have a physical form at all but can still sting you, like jellyfish.

All this brings up more questions for you to ask yourself about your monster. Is it hot or cold? Hard or soft? Dry or wet? And so on. No matter what questions you ask, the very next question you should answer is: Why?

Jellyfish use their stinging tentacles to trap prey, and those diaphanous bodies can only have evolved in the water. Crabs and insects grow their skeletons on the outside, so they're hard and bony. Humans are warm-blooded so they feel warm to the touch. Other animals are cold-blooded and will feel warm if the environment is warm, cold if the environment is cold. The nature of the monster will provide clues to what it might feel like.

WHAT DOES IT TASTE LIKE?

Okay, this last one might be tough.

We taste things only after a thorough inspection with our other senses. Though this may not be true for toddlers, who are okay with putting even the foulest things in their mouths, the rest of us are cautious about what we introduce to the inside of our bodies. If something looks poisonous, smells rotten, or makes any sound other than *snap, crackle,* and *pop*, we won't eat it.

But consider that famous scene from the movie *Ghostbusters* where Bill Murray is "slimed." He gets some of the goo in his mouth and seems intent on spitting it out. In the movie we have to assume it tastes bad—I'd rather not taste it to be sure—but in prose fiction, written from that character's POV, you'll want to describe the taste of ectoplasm.

The considerable challenge of appealing to this fifth sense is not only occasionally taken up by a brave author but sometimes pulled off with considerable aplomb, as in this brilliant excerpt from Eleanor Arnason's short story "The Woman Who Fooled Death Five Times."

> When the Goddess built the world, she worked like a good cook making a meal, tasting as she went along. She tasted the fruit to make sure it was sweet and the bitter herbs to make sure they were bitter. She tried other things as well: rocks, clay, water, bugs, fish, birds, and animals with fur. Cooked or raw, everything went onto her tongue.
>
> In the end, the world was done and seemed more than adequate. As for the Goddess, she felt bloated and over-full.

And then ... what happens when all five of our senses fail? We're talking about things that come from some imaginary place and time, and those places may not have the same rules of physics and chemistry that Earth has.

In "The Damned Thing," Ambrose Bierce imagined just such a creature:

> "As with sounds, so with colors. At each end of the solar spectrum the chemist can detect the presence of what are known as 'actinic' rays. They represent colors—integral colors in the composition of light—which we are unable to discern. The human eye is an imperfect instrument; its range is but a few octaves of the real 'chromatic scale.' I am not mad; there are colors that we cannot see.
>
> "And, God help me! the Damned Thing is of such a color!"

CHAPTER 19

STAGING THE REVEAL

Monsters are scariest when they're revealed in pieces, and scarier still when revealed slowly.

Let's look at part of that process from the novel *Cujo* by Stephen King. Quite well into the book, men delivering a chainfall (a hoisting device) encounter the possessed Saint Bernard, Cujo. The monster dog growls menacingly at them, but they get away. When they talk about it, they say the dog is "going bad," but they fail to call in a warning.

> He hadn't seen a beware of dog sign when they drove up, but sometimes these bumpkins from the boonies didn't bother with one. He knew one thing. He hoped to God that the dog making that sound was chained up.[1]

What follows is a lot of story in between monster dog scenes. Like all effective genre novels, *Cujo* is primarily a book about people. A bit less than thirty pages later, Brett (the young hero of the novel) encounters his beloved dog, Cujo, and senses that something's wrong. It's something in Cujo's eyes, and the scene that follows is about the emotional, psychological effect of the encounter more than the gooey stuff described here.

> The Saint Bernard's big, sad eyes were now reddish and stupid and lowering: more pig's eyes than dog's eyes. His coat was

---

1 *Cujo* by Stephen King, ©1981 Stephen King

plated with brownish-green mud, as if he had been rolling around in the boggy place at the bottom of the meadow. His muzzle was wrinkled back in a terrible mock grin that froze Brett with horror. Brett felt his heart slugging in his throat.

Thick white foam dripped slowly from between Cujo's teeth.

Cujo's eyes change throughout the book—in the above paragraph, they're "reddish and stupid" and later they're "leaking some viscous substance"—an indication of the dog's transformation as he evolves. And his coat is soaked with more and more blood.

Also, Cujo is consistently introduced to characters via sound.

He turned to go back in, and that was when he heard the growling begin. It was a low, powerful sound coming from just beyond the point where his overgrown side yard merged with the hayfield beyond it.

The sound Cujo makes changes from a growl to "a series of heavy, grinding sounds" to "more savage than any barks."

Considering again the idea of writing in close-up, look at how King keeps a very tight POV on the victim by pacing the action with short sentences, as in this paragraph from the book.

Gary got shakily to his feet. He backed up the last two steps of the porch. He backed across the porch's width and felt behind him for the handle of the screen door. His shoulder felt as if raw gasoline had been poured under the skin. His mind raved at him, Rabies! I got the rabies!

That's fifty-six words in six sentences. The longest sentence is seventeen words. The shortest is four words. But later, on that same page, is another single paragraph.

He turned and headed down the darkened hallway to the closet, and that was when Cujo smashed through the lower half of the screen door, muzzle wrinkled back from his teeth in a sneer, a dry volley of barking sounds coming from his chest.

This whole paragraph is one long sentence of forty-four words. Longer sentences don't give your readers a chance to catch their breaths. Don't believe me? Read them both aloud. Then think about the last time you were really scared; maybe you were in actual danger. Did you hold your breath? Did you find it hard to breathe when things were at their most dangerous? And in the moments leading up to that, when you were concentrating on what might happen, you were likely taking lots of short, sharp breaths.

THE THREE STAGES

Reveal your monsters in three stages. The first and third will be the fastest (using the least number of words) and perhaps most dramatic. The middle section is where you'll spend time revealing aspects of the monster—what it can do, what it looks, sounds, smells, and feels like— while always increasing the danger to your characters and upping the stakes for your story.

We'll look at a few different examples to illustrate this. And with the help of veteran fantasy author Lynn Abbey, we'll fall back on *Jaws* as a primary—and exceptional—example.

Although great white sharks really do exist, *Jaws* is still a monster movie because the shark doesn't act like a real shark. In fact the shark experts in that movie (Hooper and Quint) comment on its strange behavior throughout. As the story progresses viewers see a little more of the shark, a little more, a little more, and only in the very end do they see the shark from nose to tail fin.

Stage 1: First Encounter

"Early on (no later than the third chapter)," Lynn Abbey advises, "you'll need to tell the reader what the story's about."

Jaws doesn't waste much time doing this and opens from the shark's POV. Something is swimming through dark ocean waters. Then a girl runs into the water for a late-night swim. We see her from below in cutaways, but once the shark attacks, we see only what's happening above the dark water. There's no shark, no fin, nothing but the terrifying effect of something grabbing onto this poor girl. We're not even sure exactly what it's doing to her. This ambiguity keeps readers and viewers on the edge of their seats.

Chelsea Quinn Yarbro says that her absolute favorite movie monster is "whatever is making those smoking footprints in *Curse of the Demon* because in showing so little, it engages the individual fears of the audience, and each can build in their minds the most horrifying thing each can think of. Horror thrives on ambiguity, terror responds to more defined threats."

Frank Herbert's brilliant 1964 science fiction classic *Dune* again shows us the effect of the monster as seen from a certain distance, where ambiguity mixes with well-justified fear.

> Flecks of dust shadowed the sand around the crawler now. The big machine began to tip down to the right. A gigantic sand whirlpool began forming there to the right of the crawler. It moved faster and faster. Sand and dust filled the air now for hundreds of meters around.
>
> Then they saw it!
>
> A wide hole emerged from the sand. Sunlight flashed from glistening white spokes within it. The hole's diameter was at least twice the length of the crawler, Paul estimated. He watched as the machine slid into that opening in a billow of dust and sand. The hole pulled back.
>
> "Gods, what a monster!" muttered a man beside Paul.

You may not be able to see the entire monster in this excerpt, or in the early stages of *Jaws*, but you know *something* is there ... and it's dangerous.

Stage 2: The Growing Threat

This is where the bulk of your story will take place. Here you raise the stakes for your characters, steadily increasing the threat to them in the same way Stephen King did in *Cujo*, with the slow transformation of the dog into a monster.

We can find another concise example from King in his novella *The Mist*. The first we see of a monster is just a tentacle, hinting at a much larger beast outside, but as the story progresses the monsters keep getting weirder and bigger and scarier and stranger, and more and more people die and reveal terrible secrets about themselves. So the idea is that more and more of these monsters are coming and they're getting bigger and scarier and more powerful and smarter in some ways, and they have a greater impact upon us each time. The stakes are being raised, and the danger to the characters increases as well.

This leaves your readers thinking, *What next? When does this stop? When is the other shoe going to drop?* Your readers have to know you're not going to stop teasing them, that it's just going to get scarier as you go along, which is always better than going the other direction!

Science fiction and fantasy author David Drake is a fan of the original *King Kong*. "Not primarily for Kong, though, but rather the Brontosaurus as the detachment poles its raft across the swamp. The first distant appearance isn't frightening. The second appearance out of the water within twenty feet is shocking—but then the head and neck submerge again. The viewer—and the raft's crew—know exactly what's going to happen next, but you're given a few seconds to stew before the creature comes up under the raft and scatters it and the crew.

"That's a tremendous scene. I cannot praise it too highly."

This escalation reminds me of an interview I once saw with Alfred Hitchcock, in which he described the difference between horror and terror. If you show four men sitting around a table and a bomb suddenly goes off, blowing the men to bits, you get a few seconds of abject horror. But if you start with a close-up of the bomb, then slowly pan up to reveal that it's strapped to the underside of a table around which four men are playing cards, and they seem to have no idea it's there, that terror can be sustained for a long time.

But moments of abject horror can certainly heighten the effect of the terror a monster provides, especially in this second stage of the reveal. Balance is key here. Or, as Lynn Abbey suggests in regard to *Jaws*, "Periodically dole out some scary stuff (another swimmer gets eaten), some wrong-headed stuff (stupid people go shark hunting), and some misdirection (they kill a shark, but not the shark). Ham-handedly, the victims in these moments are the Red Shirts," or the characters that bite the bullet to remind readers and viewers that this situation or monster is both deadly and scary. An example in *Jaws* is a fisherman who ties a slab of meat to a rickety pier to lure the shark ... and he almost becomes a meal himself.

"Change-ups can also be useful," Abbey continues. "Once Hooper finds the shark tooth in the wrecked fishing boat, everyone's expecting the shark; no one's expecting the fisherman's head."

But it's not just about sprinkling in death and destruction. As Abbey states, "It's also the little things: objects, habits, or offhand revelations. Captain Brody's afraid of water so, of course, not only is he on a boat heading into the climax, he's in the water during and after it."

Filter in these little bits of information as the story progresses. Ask yourself what little detail about the monster (or main characters) you need to make this scene effective, and stop there. Reveal no more than necessary.

Stage 3: The Tipping Point

As we mentioned before, most monster stories reach a tipping point when a monster stops being a total mystery and the protagonist and other characters take charge of the situation. This is the point at which characters have figured out what the monster can do, what it can't do, what it wants, and so on, and they're switching into action mode. And it's okay to go into that mode, although you don't always have to. You may not want your hero to actually rise to the occasion and figure out how to turn the tables on that monster and reclaim his apex predator standing—there is something to be said for the "everybody dies at the end" ending.

But even then, there has to be a point at which characters start to act rather than react—we're still scared of this thing, but we have to try to do something about it one way or another.

"Once all the pieces are in place and the characters are en route to their inevitable climax, mess with the readers' heads," Abbey advises. "They probably think they know what you're going to do next. Disabuse them of that notion—find a way to show them the barrels without the music cue they've come to rely upon.

"Finally, wait as long as possible to reveal your monster."

In his book *Killing Monsters: Why Children Need Fantasy, Super Heroes, and Make-Believe Violence*, author Gerard Jones makes a convincing case that kids not only like to see heroes overcome the threat of monsters, but actually need those stories to help them process both the very real dangers and the perceived dangers of the grown-up world. Experiencing the defeat of a monster in fiction helps take away the monster's power.

If you've built your monster in a carefully considered, plausible way; ramped up the danger throughout the story; and found a convincing and active way for your hero to overcome that threat, you have a solid, satisfying story.

Unless, of course, you want everyone to die in the end.

It happens.

CHAPTER 20

ISOLATION

We're trapped in here with a monster, and there's no way to call for help!

How often can a monster story be reduced to that simple statement? The monster changes from story to story, and so does the definition of "in here," but the concept is the same: How do we isolate people?

Novelist Alan Dean Foster asserts that isolation is "only important in the context of the story. Monsters in a metropolis also works. But the more isolated a person, the more immediate the fear and apprehension one experiences."

In most cases if a monster attacks and someone calls 911, the police show up in a few minutes. Even if this monster is terribly weird and dangerous, it becomes their problem now. They'll call for backup, then the SWAT Team, then the National Guard, and now the story isn't hero versus monster, it's military-industrial complex versus monster. Monster stories from *Godzilla* to *The Mist* have widened the experience of the monster from a very small number of isolated people to the armed struggle of an entire nation against an invasion of dangerous creatures. And while those stories can work on a certain level, there's a reason why some of the best monsters attack a ship in deep space, a remote research base in Antarctica, a cabin in the woods, or just about anywhere during a storm, a blackout, etc. Isolation can enhance the feeling of impending doom.

To get a sense of the deep-seated unease with which we consider isolation, especially the threat of being all alone to face a possibly superior predator, we'll briefly reexamine the points made in Chapter 2, "What Makes Monsters Scary?"

Humans have evolved from primitive pack hunters with animalistic, predatory instincts to civilized beings that depend upon complex creative brains and nimble fingers to survive. These advantages allow us to make things and use those things with extraordinary precision. We also get together in groups. One guy with a rifle is dangerous. Ten thousand guys with rifles can change the course of history. And we've also invented ways to use our technology to help us get together in groups and stay together. Information technology allows us to call in reinforcements—at least call the police, or maybe even just a friend to come and help.

But take all that away ...

If you want to put your characters in a scary, dangerous situation, start stripping them of their evolutionary weapons, one by one, like pulling the fangs from a lion. And toy with our primitive instinct to stick together. Especially if the characters know that help isn't coming ...

In William Hope Hodgson's 1908 classic *The House on the Borderland*, everything that happens in the story hinges on the fact that the eponymous house is located somewhere on the edge of civilization. Scream all you want to. The neighbors can't hear you.

> I am an old man. I live here in this ancient house, surrounded by huge, unkempt gardens.
>
> The peasantry, who inhabit the wilderness beyond, say that I am mad. That is because I will have nothing to do with them. I live here alone with my old sister, who is also my housekeeper. We keep no servants—I hate them. I have one friend, a dog; yes, I would sooner have old Pepper than the rest of Creation together. He, at least, understands me—and has sense enough to leave me alone when I am in my dark moods.
>
> I have decided to start a kind of diary; it may enable me to record some of the thoughts and feelings that I cannot express to anyone; but, beyond this, I am anxious to make some record

of the strange things that I have heard and seen, during many years of loneliness, in this weird old building.

A sense of isolation is a continuing theme throughout the book, and the dramatic tension grows as the protagonist's degree of isolation deepens and his mind begins to play tricks on him:

> As I stood there, anxiously, my foot dislodged a pebble, which fell inward, into the dark, with a hollow chink. At once, the noise was taken up and repeated a score of times; each succeeding echo being fainter, and seeming to travel away from me, as though into remote distance. Then, as the silence fell again, I heard that stealthy breathing. For each respiration I made, I could hear an answering breath. The sounds appeared to be coming nearer; and then, I heard several others; but fainter and more distant. Why I did not grip the rope, and spring up out of danger, I cannot say. It was as though I had been paralyzed. I broke out into a profuse sweat, and tried to moisten my lips with my tongue. My throat had gone suddenly dry, and I coughed, huskily. It came back to me, in a dozen, horrible, throaty tones, mockingly. I peered, helplessly, into the gloom; but still nothing showed. I had a strange, choky sensation, and again I coughed, dryly. Again the echo took it up, rising and falling, grotesquely, and dying slowly into a muffled silence.
>
> Then, suddenly, a thought came to me, and I held my breath. The other breathing stopped. I breathed again, and, once more, it re-commenced. But now, I no longer feared. I knew that the strange sounds were not made by any lurking Swine-creature; but were simply the echo of my own respirations.

There are virtually infinite ways to isolate your characters, limited entirely by your imagination—and maybe the limits of your genre and subgenre of choice.

The big elephant in the room now, if you're writing a contemporary story—horror, urban fantasy, near-future science fiction—is what happens if your characters actually can just pick up their cell phones and call 911? If this is a contemporary story in which everyone has a cell phone, you'll have to figure out how to get rid of those. The cell phone has become a challenge to writers across most genres, and if you keep your eyes open, you'll see the inevitable scene in which, one way or another, cell phones are dispensed with. Batteries die, reception is poor, phones break or are left behind on purpose.

In *The Cabin in the Woods*, filmmakers Joss Whedon and Drew Goddard had a lot of fun with the well-travelled monster movie trope that begins with characters going on vacation to a secluded cabin. They've rented this cabin out in the middle of nowhere and are going there because there are no phones and no television reception. They're going there to "get away from it all" ... and then everything goes horribly awry.

Isolation is a lot easier to handle in a historical or fantasy setting. As long as you assume that nobody has a pervasive magic that subs in for cell phones, you begin with an everyday isolation we haven't had to deal with since the invention of the telephone, the radio, and so on. If you set your fantasy characters on their torturous trek from here to there, they have to cross through the Haunted Forest and they can't just call and have the rangers get them out of a tight spot. Every monster they encounter will be entirely up to them to dispose of. From the beginning they have to deal with any problems that arise on their own.

And sometimes it can be the monsters themselves that drive us into the unknown. Look at how H.P. Lovecraft's careful choice of words in "The Dream-Quest of Unknown Kadath" gives this alien landscape a terrifying sense of isolation.

> As the band flew lower the Peaks of Throk rose grey and towering on all sides, and one saw clearly that nothing lived on that austere and impressive granite of the endless twilight. At still lower levels the death-fires in the air gave out, and one met only the primal blackness of the void save aloft where the thin peaks stood out goblin-like. Soon the peaks were very

far away, and nothing about but great rushing winds with the dankness of nethermost grottoes in them. Then in the end the night-gaunts landed on a floor of unseen things which felt like layers of bones, and left Carter all alone in that black valley. To bring him thither was the duty of the night-gaunts that guard Ngranek; and this done, they flapped away silently. When Carter tried to trace their flight he found he could not, since even the Peaks of Throk had faded out of sight. There was nothing anywhere but blackness and horror and silence and bones.

Is it possible to feel any more remote than that last line?

But like the protagonist of *The House on the Borderland*, some characters themselves may *seek out* isolation, which, no matter how much we may struggle against it, will eventually drive people crazy. Humans are social animals, and the more we cut ourselves off from our fellow man, the more we risk becoming monsters ourselves.

"Catherine Deneuve's character was pretty damn isolated in [the 1965 film] *Repulsion*, leading to great horror," Scott Allie points out. "Walter White isolated himself more and more in *Breaking Bad*. We're all isolated ... and horror can explore that in terrific ways."

CHAPTER 21

ORIGINALITY: CLICHÉ VS. ARCHETYPE

Richard Baker, award-winning game designer and best-selling author of *Condemnation*, defines cliché as "the same treatment of the same idea or premise. Sometimes you want to use the power of a cliché to help tell your story: Everybody knows how werewolves or vampires work, after all. But it seems that every werewolf you see is a reluctant fellow horrified by what he does when the moon's out, and every vampire nowadays is a heart-sick immortal hundreds of years old. Time for new takes on those ideas."

Indeed.

Dragons, aliens, zombies, ghosts, demons, and loads more monsters are archetypes—these are genre staples that are available to us all. There's nothing stopping you from writing a story featuring any of these creatures, but what keeps an archetype from becoming a cliché depends on how much originality, effort, and creativity you put into it. I don't generally like vampires, but I liked *30 Days of Night* and *Let Me In* because their vampires were unique and original.

The vampires in *30 Days of Night* were both intelligent and pathologically violent, acting almost like some kind of rebel biker gang or thrill-kill cult, whereas the vampire in *Let Me In* was a little girl who was first portrayed as a sad, lonely victim and is soon revealed to be a creature of twisted, demonic evil. There wasn't a lovelorn count to be seen in either. Those stories had something to say and dipped into the expected only enough to make sure the vampires were identifiable as vampires, then went off in their own directions.

"Anything can become a cliché if it is not understood by those writing about it," said Chelsea Quinn Yarbro, author of the Saint-Germaine novels, a successful—and original—vampire series. "In vampire and were-being stories, the writer will do better if she or he decides what the vampire or were-being represents, and what interactions with the more normally alive will bring. Once those two decisions have been made, then the writer must take care to adhere to those rules, no matter how inconvenient. A writer will need to research the vampire and/or were-creature archetype—for vampires, I recommend Anthony Masters's *The Natural History of the Vampire*. It's an excellent survey on folklore, literature, and film. Watching Hammer films and re-runs of *Buffy* are a lot of fun, but neither is research and will not sustain new tales."

Or as Scott Allie of Dark Horse Comics put it, a monster becomes a cliché "if we feel we've seen it too many times. To me the most boring stuff is a really overwrought design, probably riffing on Giger's Alien, but without any mystery or story. The worst cliché is when you copy something you love without any understanding of why everyone else loved it."

So a cliché is simply a badly rendered archetype, devoid of a spark of individual life. But how can you start with an archetype and avoid cliché?

THE MONSTER MIXING BOARD

Everybody's looking for the next Harry Potter, but if you take that as "I have a copy of Harry Potter in my left hand and a pen in my right hand," that's not at all what I mean. When I say they're looking for the next Harry Potter, I mean they're looking for the next new thing like Harry Potter—a book that comes out of nowhere and touches a nerve with a huge crossover audience.

Harry Potter borrows traits, archetypes, and themes from all over the place—a lot of stuff that comes out of the established fantasy and fairy tale lexicon—but it was mixed together with this weird alchemy that was different from anything else happening at the time. That's what they mean by wanting another Harry Potter—not literally the next Harry Potter, but the next entirely different thing that works like Harry Potter. And we've already seen that happen in the young reader sphere with the Twilight series, then The Hunger Games trilogy, neither of which were much like Harry Potter at all.

Think about fantasy, science fiction, and horror archetypes like vampires in terms of a series of dials, like on a recording studio mixing board. Each knob represents some aspect of the traditional vampire: drinks blood, destroyed by sunlight, repelled by crosses, etc., and you can adjust those knobs in a range from zero to a hundred.

Are your vampires instantly destroyed by the slightest touch of sunlight? Then set that dial to maximum. Perhaps you'd rather they can go out in the daytime, but they just aren't as powerful when they do, or maybe they're prone to nasty sunburns after a short exposure. Set that dial to twenty or thirty. Or just turn that dial down to zero and your vampires have no problem at all with sunlight. Likewise imagine a dial for "drinks blood" where one hundred might be the most violent, throat-rending fanged maw like we saw in *30 Days of Night*; fifty is *Dracula*'s relatively delicate fangs; and the vampires of Whitely Strieber's *The Hunger*, who use small blades to cut the throats of their victims, might register in the single digits. How these dials are set is entirely up to you.

SHOPPING FOR ARCHETYPES

Draw inspiration for monsters from just about any source you like, especially since we now know to creatively alter the nature of that archetypical beastie.

What animals scare you? Spiders, snakes ... parasites? They scare author Alan Dean Foster. "I feel a kinship to most larger creatures, but anything that feeds on you without return is a true monster. Leeches straddle that divide. Mosquitoes do not."

Martin J. Dougherty says that there's "a threshold where an animal becomes a monster without necessarily gaining tentacles and spikes. If it's scary enough, it becomes a monster. Lack of understanding contributes to this, [as does] alien-ness. Wolverines are really scary, but they're just badass animals. Giant squid, on the other hand, might be monsters. An animal that is both alien and menacing? That there's a monster."

And you obviously don't have to start with an animal at all, or at least with one single animal. Monster archetypes exist that combine traits or physical structures of more than one animal, like Dungeons & Dragons's owlbear or the classical chimera, which has the head of a lion, the body of a goat, and a serpent's tail. Chelsea Quinn Yarbro finds "a lot of intriguing monsters in folklore of all sorts, and through folklore, a wonderful range of the unusual, the outré, and the frightening."

But you don't have to rely on folklore for scary monsters. The most original monsters can come from the deepest, darkest recesses of your own mind. When Lynn Abbey needs something truly monstrous, she'll "pull it directly from my nightmares—because it needs to be something that unnerves me, if I'm going to have a hope of unnerving my readers."

ORIGINALITY

Every writer has to be original—that's how you're going to get noticed. If you try to surf trends, you'll sink. Teen vampires are "hot" right now, but if you sit down and pound your way through a teen vampire book … you're in big trouble. By the time you've finished that book (or screenplay or video game) that trend will surely have burned itself out.

That doesn't mean you can't stand on the shoulders of giants and take something that has worked before and spin it into something new. Hayao Miyazaki and Guillermo del Toro are two monster makers operating on the bleeding edge, pushing fantasy way out into another new paradigm. By all means, study their work, as well as the work of your other favorite novelists, filmmakers, and game studios, but do so keeping in mind these words of caution from Guillermo del Toro (from an interview at *Co.CREATE*).[1]

> If you're trying to make a monster by imitating, say, Ray Harryhausen, then you immerse yourself in Harryhausen and find out he was inspired by the French engraver Gustav Doré. Then you find out Doré was inspired by neo-classical sculptures and engravers so you go there and little by little you wind up looking at rough fourteenth century illustrations. You see an olive-skinned devil with a face on its ass and you realize, "Oh my God this works because it's simple." You have to always try to express the creature in its purest form."

It seems old-fashioned and quaint and silly, but there are no rules, no monster police, no worldbuilding judge telling you that you have to do this and you can't do that. You can take an old idea and go anywhere you want with it. In fiction, anything can happen, and we've most certainly gotten to that point in other forms of media, too. Video games are getting weirder and more fantastic, and movies with digital effects can bring anything to life. But with so many people vying to create that next new original hit, we all have to start figuring out ways to make anything that goes into worldbuilding and storytelling that much more original.

Use all the tools available to you. You'll need 'em!

---

1 www.fastcocreate.com/3020262/master-class/guillermo-del-toro-shares-14-horror-insights-from-his-spectacular-sketch-book

GREAT MONSTERS: ALIEN

Screenwriter Dan O'Bannon first started pitching a script he called *Starbeast* in 1976. About a year later, Twentieth Century Fox found itself in the enviable position of having taken a chance on a different young writer/director, George Lucas. When *Star Wars* went from being a weird little space movie to a huge international blockbuster, Fox wanted more. *Starbeast* became *Alien* and went into production in the capable hands of director Ridley Scott. Released in 1979, right in between Steven Spielberg's much more "alien-positive" films *Close Encounters of the Third Kind* (1977) and *E.T. the Extra-Terrestrial* (1982), *Alien* presented a much less optimistic view of first contact.

The eponymous creature of *Alien* wasn't interested in synthesizer jams, riding bikes, or phoning home. Not at all.

"*Alien* confronts us with something primal and horrible: We are prey," Richard Baker says. "Not only that, *Alien* says that we're the victims of the most horrible form of predation imaginable, playing the unwilling host to another creature's reproductive cycle. It implies a whole ecosystem of wrong."

Dan O'Bannon, in an interview with David Konow,[1] said, "I wanted it to be really obvious to studio executives in 1976 that the monster was not going to be cripplingly difficult to pull off." The reason being, before *Star Wars*, budgets for science fiction movies were not necessarily a studio priority. "I wanted to write it so most of it was clearly a man in a suit..."

I'll take this moment to remind you again that if you're writing prose fiction, you don't have to worry about special effects and

---

1 "Dan O'Bannon and the Origins of *Alien*" (www.tested.com/art/movies/458897-dan-obannon-and-origins-alien)

makeup budget constraints. And even if you're writing a screenplay, the technology to create a more outré monster via digital effects will allow you to stretch your imagination a bit more than was possible in the late seventies.

But it wasn't the bipedal form of the alien that scared us so much as the way it went about making little aliens. "I modeled it after microscopic parasites that move from one animal to the next and have complex life cycles," O'Bannon told Konow. "I just enlarged a parasite. I was interested in the biology of aliens, so I wasn't interested in streamlining the thing below interest level just for the sake of economy."

Certainly the most famous (or infamous, depending on how squeamish you are) scene in the film is the one in which an unfortunate crewman who fell victim to the mysterious "facehugger" wakes up, eats, then suddenly goes into convulsions. You know what happens next ...

"I thought, well we ought to do something in here, something fairly early that is excessive," O'Bannon explained. "Something over the line. Something so awful that you just shouldn't do it. I'll just do it once, and I'll do it early enough that most of the picture still has yet to play. Then after that all you have to do is make sure there's a lot of dark shadows in the corridors as you're walking around so you can't see anything. You can stretch those scenes out until the audience's teeth will shatter into nothing waiting for the unpredictable moment where the next dreadful, unacceptable thing is hurled at you."

It's the motivation of the alien that makes it terrifying. It's not there to manipulate you or get you to do bad things. It's not going to negotiate. As Ash, the android science officer in the film, almost mockingly warns his surviving crewmates, "You still don't understand what you're dealing with, do you? A perfect organism. Its structural perfection is matched only by its hostility.

"I admire its purity. It's a survivor ... unclouded by conscience, remorse, or delusions of morality."

Martin J. Dougherty describes it as "strange, menacing, and powerful, again completely inimical to humans (in a variety of exciting new ways) and not because it got up this morning and decided to be bad, it's just being what it is. That's disturbing because it implies that there are things out there in the universe to which we are just food/incubators/chew toys; they can't be bribed, begged, or reasoned with. That sort of complete, uncaring menace is disturbing. The alien isn't even hostile as such; it's just taking advantage of food that wandered into its path."

And it remains among the scariest movie monsters in cinema history.

ARCHETYPES: ZOMBIES

The *zonbi,* or zombie, originates in Haitian folklore. In certain voodoo practices, it's said that a particularly talented sorcerer can animate the corpses of the recently dead. But the mind of the deceased doesn't come back with its body's ability to shamble around. Instead the zombie acts as a basically mindless servant of the sorcerer.

Efforts have been made to determine if there is a scientific explanation for this legend, especially since there are still the occasional "zombie sightings" in Haiti today. Researchers have looked into a combination of home-brewed drugs that create first a catatonic state nearly indistinguishable from death, followed by partial reanimation and a severe, hallucinogen-induced psychosis that could make the victim appear to be a member of the "walking dead," but that still doesn't mean there are real-life, brain- and/or flesh-eating zombies.

If anything, the closest real-world equivalent to a zombie plague is rabies. Rabies drives its victims insane while propelling them to spread the disease via bites and scratches ... and it's always fatal.

But "real" zombies aside, the undead started out playing only a small role in the horror canon, with early stories from the likes of H.P. Lovecraft that were more akin to Frankenstein than the contemporary zombie, as in Lovecraft's "Herbert West: Reanimator."

> One thing had uttered a nerve-shattering scream; another had risen violently, beaten us both to unconsciousness, and run amuck in a shocking way before it could be placed behind asylum bars; still another, a loathsome African monstrosity, had clawed out of its shallow grave and done a deed—West

had had to shoot that object. We could not get bodies fresh enough to show any trace of reason when reanimated, so had perforce created nameless horrors. It was disturbing to think that one, perhaps two, of our monsters still lived—that thought haunted us shadowingly, till finally West disappeared under frightful circumstances. But at the time of the scream in the cellar laboratory of the isolated Bolton cottage, our fears were subordinate to our anxiety for extremely fresh specimens.

It wasn't until an independent filmmaker from the most unlikely of "movie towns," Pittsburgh, Pennsylvania, got together with some friends from a local TV station and made the now-legendary indie horror classic *Night of the Living Dead* that the modern zombie was finally born.

Taking only scant inspiration from the Haitian legend, *Night of the Living Dead* imagined the zombie combined with the classic ghoul—a monster that eats the flesh of living humans—and made the source of its animation not a witch or voodoo priest but something more akin to a virulent plague.

Romero's zombies inexplicably rose from the dead with an insatiable hunger for human flesh. Anyone "fortunate" enough to be bitten but escape being totally consumed by a zombie would quickly die and become a zombie, too. Zombies make more zombies, and more zombies, and more zombies until the whole world is overrun.

Since *Night of the Living Dead* was released in 1968, a handful of sequels were made and many imitations spawned. Romero's cannibalistic zombies have become the newest and one of the most popular monster archetypes. In short, this one-time amateur filmmaker from Pittsburgh has done nothing short of creating a new shared mythology.

Of today's zombies, some follow Romero's archetype almost exactly, including the need to destroy a zombie's head or brain in order to kill it. Romero's zombies were slow moving and dim witted, but later iterations, as in the 2004 remake of Romero's *Dawn of the Dead*, gave us the so-called "fast zombie" and all sorts of controversy among zombie fandom.

The zombie, like dragons and vampires, are up for grabs, but as with any archetypical monster, look for ways to "customize" your zombies. Do you really have to destroy their brains, or can they be killed in other ways? Are they a little smarter, as we started to see in Romero's own *Day of the Dead*, or really smart as in the movie *Warm Bodies*? Or are they really victims of a sort of mutated rabies, as in the movies *28 Days Later* or *Quarantine*?

Or would you rather we took some time off from the walking dead the same way I would like to have a break from vampires? I asked Alan Dean Foster and his response was: "Zombies ... let 'em stay dead."

REAL MONSTERS: DINOSAURS

Before some large celestial object—an asteroid or comet—smashed into the Earth and led to mass extinction, our planet was a world of monsters.

While it is clear from historical records that people have discovered fossilized dinosaur bones as long as two thousand years ago, the first dinosaur identified in a modern scientific manner was named *Megalosaurus* by William Buckland in 1824, and it gave birth to the modern study of paleontology. Since then, fossil hunters have combed the Earth and discovered a once-rich ecosystem of massive creatures, some significantly bigger than the biggest land animals alive today—and some of those giants had fangs.

Paleontology is a serious scientific pursuit, and one made rather difficult by the lack of anything but fossilized remains, so it's no surprise that our conception of what certain dinosaurs were like often changes. If you're setting out to write a nonfiction book about dinosaurs, you have some serious research ahead of you, but if you're looking to grab a handy monster off the shelf of real-life creatures, you can be as sketchy as Lovecraft in "The Shadow Out of Time."

> Beyond the wide, warm ocean were other cities of the Great Race, and on one far continent I saw the crude villages of the black-snouted, winged creatures who would evolve as a dominant stock after the Great Race had sent its foremost minds into the future to escape the creeping horror. Flatness and exuberant green life were always the keynote of the scene. Hills were low and sparse, and usually displayed signs of volcanic forces.
>
> Of the animals I saw, I could write volumes. All were wild; for the Great Race's mechanised culture had long since done

away with domestic beasts, while food was wholly vegetable or synthetic. Clumsy reptiles of great bulk floundered in steaming morasses, fluttered in the heavy air, or spouted in the seas and lakes; and among these I fancied I could vaguely recognise lesser, archaic prototypes of many forms—dinosaurs, pterodactyls, ichthyosaurs, labyrinthodonts, plesiosaurs, and the like—made familiar through palaeontology. Of birds or mammals there were none that I could discover.

Many species of dinosaurs are instantly recognizable. Who can't immediately conjure up an image of a Tyrannosaurus rex or a triceratops? But if you're looking back sixty-five million years or more for inspiration, and the real science is still rapidly evolving, who says you can't put your own spin on these long-lost creatures?

Consider *Jurassic Park*[2] by Michael Crichton, the *Gone With the Wind* of dinosaur monster stories. In this scene, the hapless Nedry runs afoul of a dilophosaurus.

> The dinosaur stood forty feet away, at the edge of the illumination from the headlamps. Nedry hadn't taken the tour, so he hadn't seen the different types of dinosaurs, but this one was strange-looking. The ten-foot-tall body was yellow with black spots, and along the head ran a pair of red V-shaped crests. The dinosaur didn't move, but again gave its soft hooting cry.

But our Mr. Nedry is not so lucky, and the little dinosaur spits some kind of corrosive venom at him. At first Nedry thinks this is disgusting, but then the dinosaur spits its poison into his eyes ...

---

2 Alfred A. Knopf 1990, ©1990 Michael Crichton

Even as he realized it, the pain overwhelmed him, and he dropped to his knees, disoriented, wheezing. He collapsed onto his side, his cheek pressed to the wet ground, his breath coming in thin whistles through the constant, ever-screaming pain that caused flashing spots of light to appear behind his tightly shut eyelids.

The earth shook beneath him and Nedry knew the dinosaur was moving, he could hear its soft hooting cry, and despite the pain he forced his eyes open and still he saw nothing but flashing spots against black. Slowly the realization came to him.

He was blind.

And then the dinosaur proceeds to eat him alive.

Scary stuff to be sure, but then there appears to be no solid scientific evidence that dilophosaurus was venomous or that it had articulated neck frills, although it did live in the Jurassic period, 190–200 million years ago. The real dilophosaurus was actually much bigger than the one depicted in the movie adaptation, much closer to what Crichton specified in his book, but that choice by Steven Spielberg seems to balance out the velociraptor, which was not only much smaller than seen in the movie (between eighteen inches and two feet tall, not eight feet tall), but also likely had feathers.

In the same way that you're free to adjust the dials on what a vampire can and can't do, dinosaurs are yours to play with as you see fit, even though they were as real as any living animal. Let's put it this way: If Stephen King can make a monster out of a Saint Bernard, who says Michael Crichton can't get a dilophosaurus to spit poison?

Remember, this is fiction we're writing. Have fun.

THE CRYPTIDS: CHUPACABRA

Of all the supposed "real" monsters studied by cryptozoologists, none is weirder than the infamous "goat sucker" of Latin America. Reports of this bizarre, alien-like, canine semihumanoid—or whatever it is—began to grow in popularity in the 1990s after livestock, mostly goats, were found dead with small puncture wounds reminiscent of a vampire's bite—and all the animal's blood drained away.

Sightings began to proliferate across Mexico and Central America and even in the Caribbean, especially Puerto Rico, where the creature took on a singularly alien cast—possibly inspired by, of all things, the alien from the movie *Species*.

Eyewitness accounts describe a small creature, maybe three feet tall, standing on two legs, and with a head and face roughly like the classic alien "Grey": big eyes—red rather than the classic alien black—small nostrils but no nose to speak of, and a thin-lipped mouth. Unlike the classic alien, though, the chupacabra's back is lined with long spines and its hands are webbed and tipped with sharp claws.

In the past several years a number of farmers, hunters, and ... let's call them "adventurers" ... have captured or killed specimens of what they claim to be the chupacabra, which is more than we can say for the *Finding Bigfoot* crew. But when these animals are tested they prove to be either domestic dogs or coyotes suffering from mange, scabies, or other diseases of the skin that cause their fur to fall out. Mange can give a common coyote quite a startling—one could say "monstrous"—appearance, but that doesn't make it a monster, just a poor little coyote with a bad case of an all-too-common canine malady.

Still, once a creature like the chupacabra enters the collective consciousness it takes more than scientific evidence to dismiss it, and the "goat sucker" remains one of cryptozoology's favorite catchalls. The chupacabra is thought to be everything from a feral animal of an as-yet unidentified species, like Bigfoot, to some kind of transdimensional or extraterrestrial intelligence—or even some combination of both.

But for our purposes, it's a scary little thing that hides in the desert, hunting prey, desperate for blood—a monstrous vampire that may or may not be possessed of humanlike cunning. Your chupacabra can be anything from a misunderstood natural predator to a mutated, diseased, or zombified alien. Inspiration galore is just an online search away.

Let the goat sucking begin!

MONSTROUS THINGS: THE BOMB

The first nuclear fission bomb, which the scientists who created it called simply "The Gizmo," was detonated on July 16, 1945. Only three weeks later, another similar device, nicknamed "Little Boy," was detonated in the sky over the Japanese city of Hiroshima, instantly vaporizing everything in a half-mile diameter at ground zero and killing sixty-six thousand people in an instant.

I can't think of a single science fiction or fantasy monster that's done more damage more quickly.

But does the atomic bomb qualify as a monster? Remember: *A monster is any creature of a species that is neither a part of the civilization of sentient people or among the ranks of mundane flora and fauna.*

For best-selling author Richard Baker, "The Bomb is only truly monstrous when taken as a metaphor for the human impulse toward self-destruction, as it is portrayed in *Dr. Strangelove* or *Beneath the Planet of the Apes.*"

So then, in a way, it is a monster the same way that a zombie horde is a monster. It's a disaster—the very presence of the thing, as much as the aftereffects of its use—that brings out the good or evil in people. And, wow, does it ever function as a metaphor.

But does The Bomb have to be a nuclear weapon?

"It's not impossible that The Bomb could be something other than a nuclear weapon," Lynn Abbey says, "but readers would come to the story with expectations that could be hard to dislodge. More to the point, I'd find it difficult to dislodge my own memories. I could write a story about lying awake at night, being afraid that The Bomb would drop before my father got home from work ... but that would be a memoir, not a novel."

In many ways, the threat of nuclear annihilation defined the Cold War years. The very real effects of the weapon on Hiroshima and Nagasaki were impossible to ignore and impossible to not find utterly terrifying. And The Bomb immediately started to conjure images of monsters. Project leader Robert Oppenheimer, "credited" as the inventor of the atomic bomb, famously quoted from the Bhagavad-Gita: "I am become Death, the destroyer of worlds," after the first test was successful. Since then we've heard nuclear weapons referred to with language usually reserved for dangerous animals: Will we unleash the nuclear threat?

In his 1953 short story, "The Variable Man," Philip K. Dick imagined a future in which Earth is locked in an endless stalemate with the enemy in our neighboring star system, Proxima Centaurus. Clever scientists develop a robotic cruise missile with one foot in the territory of weapon, and the other in a universe of monsters.

> "Icarus will be launched outside the lab, on the surface. He will align himself with Proxima Centaurus, gaining speed rapidly. By the time he reaches his destination he will be traveling at FTL-100. Icarus will be brought back to this universe within Centaurus itself. The explosion should destroy the star and wash away most of its planets—including their central hub-planet, Armun. There is no way they can halt Icarus, once he has been launched. No defense is possible. Nothing can stop him. It is a real fact."
>
> "When will he be ready?"
>
> Sherikov's eyes flickered. "Soon."

And in that story, Philip K. Dick is less interested in the nature of The Bomb itself than in the all-too-human willingness, or reluctance, to use it. With The Bomb, the idea is that this "monster" can bring out the evil in people who might use it to destroy thousands, even millions of people in a flash, rather than killing off a few teenagers in a remote cabin in the woods. And if that evil character can amass enough of these devices, he can kill us all. That raises the stakes of how human characters react to this monster-as-disaster to the very highest level: global annihilation.

CONCLUSION

MONSTERS FOREVER!

Monsters are as popular as ever. And they're everywhere. Monsters are crawling all over movies, television, books, graphic novels and comic books, video games, smart phone apps ... in every form of media out there.

But why?

When I asked Dark Horse Comics' writer Scott Allie why we love monsters, he told me, "Because I'm not so sure of my love of humans. Monsters help me understand that."

In his book *Killing Monsters: Why Children Need Fantasy, Super Heroes, and Make-Believe Violence*,[1] Gerard Jones offered these words of advice on the relationship between kids and violent media, and for me, the same goes for adults.

> We've been taught to fear stories. Popular articles, teacher train-
> ing programs, handouts from pediatricians often list "an interest
> in violent stories or entertainment" as one of the warning signs
> that a child has the potential for violent behavior. And violent
> kids are interested in such things. But so are many of the kids
> who are trying mightily to take control of their feelings of anger
> and powerlessness without violence. If kids bully other kids, hit
> or verbally abuse their girlfriends or boyfriends, or explode over
> small slights; if they show cruelty to animals or boast of cruel
> deeds or plans; if they nurse long grudges, destroy property, or
> talk or write about specific revenge fantasies against real people;

---

1 Basic Books 2002, ©2002 Gerard Jones

if they cut themselves or talk about suicide, then their fascination
for violent stories may be part of a pattern that will escalate to real
violence or self-violence. But the stories themselves are more likely
to be the ways they speak their feelings and hope for us to listen.

Children's book author Nina Hess sums it up like this: "Monsters are a
little scary, but not too scary. They give kids a thrill of being scared but
within the context of a safe place, like a book or movie. Being scared is
entertaining! Also monsters are cool looking and powerful. When you
are a kid, you have so little power over your own circumstances that
there's something irresistible about creatures who hold sway over just
about anyone. Why do kids like dinosaurs? Or tigers? Same reason."

I grew up on monsters and turned out just fine—more than fine, actually. I grew up in tune with my imagination, curious about the world
around me, fascinated by subjects like science and history—all fodder
for stories of heroes and villains, rocket ships and robots, and more than
anyone's fair share of monsters.

And now the gauntlet has been thrown down to challenge this gen-
eration's imagination. Monsters are getting weirder. In fact, everything's
getting weirder, because everybody is looking for that original space to
inhabit—and maybe that space is in the strangely metaphorical fairy
tale universe of Miyazaki or the unsettling nightmare world of del Toro.
Maybe it's a new combination of familiar elements that gave us *Twilight* or *Cloverfield*, but as technology has improved how monsters can
be brought to life, have our imaginations in some way lagged behind?

Fantasy, science fiction, and horror alike can be very conservative.
And I don't mean in the Fox News sense of the word. In many ways, at
least on the publishing side, fantasy is too often about staying inside
this little box we live in. You have to be medieval and you have to have a
king and then the princess is in trouble and the hero has to go save the
princess—that all-too-familiar quest fantasy that more or less plays out
in the same way: First we build a fellowship of like-minded individuals,
then we go out to fight the bad guy.

Science fiction often puts far too much emphasis on science over fiction in an increasingly cynical way that doesn't match the exuberance of most science fiction filmmaking. Remember when reading science fiction was fun? It's been a while, frankly.

Or even the standard approach to horror. By now we know what people are afraid of: clowns and children. And if you actually look through Stephen King's entire catalog, as brilliant as his is, many of his monsters tend to be children. And I don't think it's weird that Stephen King is a father. Most fathers are terrified of their children in a roundabout way—I know I am.

Alien is as much about the fear of childbirth as it is the fear of a superior predator. This thing explodes out of you in pain and blood and gore and then destroys your whole family and screws up your house and destroys your livelihood. Children can be terribly scary, and men, who don't go through the process of childbirth and who don't have that biological urge to accept that this is happening to them, must learn to nurture this weird thing that's popped out all bloody and gross. And imagine how women must feel who go through the process in a much more physical way! On a certain level, children are just bundles of responsibility that continuously demand things and eat and eat and eat until you're broke. Then they reach the age at which they want to take care of themselves but can't, and they tell you you're bogus and you're an idiot and slam their bedroom doors and you have to find your wife and say, "Good, that was a great plan we had, having children. Let's go back and rethink that plan."

But I love my children for the same reason I love monsters, because they scare the crap out of me and surprise me and delight me and entertain me and inspire my creativity.

And see what I did there? I cast my own children as monsters, because monsters aren't about how weird an animal can be, they're about what scares and excites and delights us. They're lessons, fables, teachers, and warnings. And even as we wander into an age where our imaginations can be more richly realized, our monsters are already starting to look different, but the best of them are still created by individuals with something to say.

What will your monsters tell us about you?

"THE UNNAMABLE"

BY H.P. LOVECRAFT

This classic monster story was written in September 1923 and published in the July 1925 issue of the famed pulp magazine *Weird Tales*. The writing is classic Lovecraft—more than a bit dated, even overwrought by today's standards—and yet it remains a staple of the genre. We've seen some terrific examples drawn from Lovecraft's writing; now let's read one of his complete stories to see how some of the things we've discussed can come together to make a whole.

We were sitting on a dilapidated seventeenth century tomb in the late afternoon of an autumn day at the old burying ground in Arkham, and speculating about the unnamable. Looking toward the giant willow in the cemetery, whose trunk had nearly engulfed an ancient, illegible slab, I had made a fantastic remark about the spectral and unmentionable nourishment which the colossal roots must be sucking from that hoary, charnel earth; when my friend chided me for such nonsense and told me that since no interments had occurred there for over a century, nothing could possibly exist to nourish the tree in other than an ordinary manner. Besides, he added, my constant talk about "unnamable" and "unmentionable" things was a very puerile device, quite in keeping with my lowly standing as an author.[1] I was too fond of ending my stories with sights or sounds which paralyzed my heroes' faculties and left them without courage, words, or associations to tell what they had experienced. We know things, he said, only through our five senses or our intuitions; wherefore it is quite impossible to refer to any object or spectacle which cannot be clearly depicted by the solid definitions of fact or the correct doctrines of theology—preferably those of the Congregationalist, with whatever modifications tradition and Sir Arthur Conan Doyle may supply.[2]

With this friend, Joel Manton, I had often languidly disputed. He was principal of the East High School, born and bred in Boston and sharing New England's self-satisfied deafness to the delicate overtones of life. It was his view that only our normal, objective experiences possess any esthetic significance, and that it is the province of the artist not so much to rouse strong emotion by action, ecstasy, and astonishment, as to maintain a placid interest and appreciation by accurate, detailed transcripts of everyday affairs. Especially did he object to my preoccupation with the mystical and the unexplained; for although believing in the supernatural much more fully than I, he would not admit that it is sufficiently commonplace for literary treatment. That a mind can find its greatest pleasure in escapes

---

1 This is an interestingly self-referential point for H.P. Lovecraft to make, having been widely criticized—and just as beloved—for his colorful adjectives. Lovecraft scholars have compiled lists of some of his "favorite" words, many of which you'll find in Appendix A.

2 Here Lovecraft is making a point that we've explored in detail: How do people perceive the world around them? After all, both our readers and our characters are people and share these same senses. But at the same time, Lovecraft is describing the very thing that's made his work stand out for decades. He mentions the psychological, emotional, and spiritual effect that his monsters have on his characters, leaving suspect his friend's assertion that we experience the world around us only as dispassionate observers.

from the daily treadmill, and in original and dramatic recombinations of images usually thrown by habit and fatigue into the hackneyed patterns of actual existence, was something virtually incredible to his clear, practical, and logical intellect. With him all things and feelings had fixed dimensions, properties, causes, and effects; and although he vaguely knew that the mind sometimes holds visions and sensations of far less geometrical, classifiable, and workable nature, he believed himself justified in drawing an arbitrary line and ruling out of court all that cannot be experienced and understood by the average citizen. Besides, he was almost sure that nothing can be really "unnamable." It didn't sound sensible to him.[3]

Though I well realized the futility of imaginative and metaphysical arguments against the complacency of an orthodox sun-dweller, something in the scene of this afternoon colloquy moved me to more than usual contentiousness. The crumbling slate slabs, the patriarchal trees, and the centuried gambrel roofs of the witch-haunted old town that stretched around, all combined to rouse my spirit in defense of my work; and I was soon carrying my thrusts into the enemy's own country. It was not, indeed, difficult to begin a counterattack, for I knew that Joel Manton actually half clung to many old wives' superstitions which sophisticated people had long outgrown; beliefs in the appearance of dying persons at distant places, and in the impressions left by old faces on the windows through which they

---

3 Nina Hess, the *New York Times* best-selling author of *A Practical Guide to Monsters*, thinks that "monsters embody many universal fears and desires—and the lore of monsters taps into the need to address those universal emotions." Monsters, in that sense, help us organize who we are, who we want to be, and what we're afraid of in ourselves and others.

had gazed all their lives.[4] To credit these whisperings of rural grandmothers, I now insisted, argued a faith in the existence of spectral substances on the earth apart from and subsequent to their material counterparts. It argued a capability of believing in phenomena beyond all normal notions; for if a dead man can transmit his visible or tangible image half across the world, or down the stretch of the centuries, how can it be absurd to suppose that deserted houses are full of queer sentient things, or that old graveyards teem with the terrible, unbodied intelligence of generations? And since spirit, in order to cause all the manifestations attributed to it, cannot be limited by any of the laws of matter, why is it extravagant to imagine psychically living dead things in shapes—or absences of shapes—which must for human spectators be utterly and appallingly "unnamable"? "Common sense" in reflecting on these subjects, I assured my friend with some warmth, is merely a stupid absence of imagination and mental flexibility.

Twilight had now approached, but neither of us felt any wish to cease speaking. Manton seemed unimpressed by my arguments, and eager to refute them, having that confidence in his own opinions which had doubtless caused his success as a teacher; whilst I was too sure of my ground to fear defeat. The dusk fell, and lights faintly gleamed in some of the distant windows, but we did not move. Our seat on the tomb was very comfortable, and I knew that my prosaic friend would not mind the cavernous rift in the ancient, root-disturbed brickwork close behind us, or the utter blackness of the

---

4 Take note of how Lovecraft skillfully yet playfully wrote around the word *ghost*. We know exactly what he means, but he invokes the creepiness of the idea of a ghost rather than simply stating, "My friend believes in ghosts."

spot brought by the intervention of a tottering, deserted seventeenth century house between us and the nearest lighted road. There in the dark, upon that riven tomb by the deserted house, we talked on about the "unnamable" and after my friend had finished his scoffing I told him of the awful evidence behind the story at which he had scoffed the most.

My tale had been called "The Attic Window," and appeared in the January, 1922, issue of Whispers. In a good many places, especially the South and the Pacific coast, they took the magazines off the stands at the complaints of silly milk-sops; but New England didn't get the thrill and merely shrugged its shoulders at my extravagance. The thing, it was averred, was biologically impossible to start with; merely another of those crazy country mutterings which Cotton Mather[5] had been gullible enough to dump into his chaotic *Magnalia Christi Americana*, and so poorly authenticated that even he had not ventured to name the locality where the horror occurred. And as to the way I amplified the bare jotting of the old mystic—that was quite impossible, and characteristic of a flighty and notional scribbler! Mather had indeed told of the thing as being born, but nobody but a cheap sensationalist would think of having it grow up, look into people's windows at night, and be hidden in the attic of a house, in flesh and in spirit, till someone saw it at the window centuries later and couldn't describe what it was that turned his hair gray. All this was flagrant trashiness, and my friend Manton was not slow to insist on that fact. Then I told him what I had found in an old diary kept between 1706

---

5 Cotton Mather (1663–1728) was an influential Puritan minister who some believe served as a sort of spiritual leader of the infamous Salem Witch Trials. In this reference Lovecraft begins to ground "The Unnamable" in a historical context.

and 1723, unearthed among family papers not a mile from where we were sitting; that, and the certain reality of the scars on my ancestor's chest and back which the diary described.[6] I told him, too, of the fears of others in that region, and how they were whispered down for generations; and how no mythical madness came to the boy who in 1793 entered an abandoned house to examine certain traces suspected to be there.

It had been an eldritch[7] thing—no wonder sensitive students shudder at the Puritan age in Massachusetts. So little is known of what went on beneath the surface—so little, yet such a ghastly festering as it bubbles up putrescently in occasional ghoulish glimpses. The witchcraft terror is a horrible ray of light on what was stewing in men's crushed brains, but even that is a trifle. There was no beauty; no freedom—we can see that from the architectural and household remains, and the poisonous sermons of the cramped divines. And inside that rusted iron straitjacket lurked gibbering hideousness, perversion, and diabolism. Here, truly, was the apotheosis of The Unnamable.[8]

Cotton Mather, in that demoniac sixth book which no one should read after dark, minced no words as he flung forth his anathema. Stern as a Jewish prophet, and laconically unamazed as none since his day could be, he told of the beast that had brought forth what was more than beast

---

6 Note that Lovecraft is describing the *effect* of this legendary monster well in advance of revealing the shape of the monster itself. Ultimately, what people fear is pain, mutilation, and death ... not scales, slime, or spikes ...

7 An obscure word, *eldritch*, but one that is well known to Lovecraft readers. It's a sixteenth-century Scottish word meaning "ghostly" or "weird."

8 Still Lovecraft is describing the *situation* surrounding the monster rather than the monster itself. In this paragraph he's put it into a social and historical context with the idea that the Puritans of New England hid some kind of terrible truth. This speaks to a shared sense that there's a rotten underbelly to even the most chaste and civilized exterior. Lovecraft was neither the first nor the last author to mine this territory.

but less than man—the thing with the blemished eye—and of the screaming drunken wretch that hanged for having such an eye. This much he baldly told, yet without a hint of what came after. Perhaps he did not know, or perhaps he knew and did not dare to tell.[9] Others knew, but did not dare to tell—there is no public hint of why they whispered about the lock on the door to the attic stairs in the house of a childless, broken, embittered old man who had put up a blank slate slab by an avoided grave, although one may trace enough evasive legends to curdle the thinnest blood.[10]

It is all in that ancestral diary I found; all the hushed innuendoes and furtive tales of things with a blemished eye seen at windows in the night or in deserted meadows near the woods. Something had caught my ancestor on a dark valley road, leaving him with marks of horns on his chest and of apelike claws on his back; and when they looked for prints in the trampled dust they found the mixed marks of split hooves and vaguely anthropoid paws.[11] Once a post-rider said he saw an old man chasing and calling to a frightful loping, nameless thing on Meadow Hill in the thinly moonlit hours before dawn, and many believed him. Certainly there was strange talk one night in 1710 when the childless, broken old man was buried in the crypt behind his own house in sight of the blank slate slab. They nev-

---

9 Here Lovecraft establishes a firm foundation for his "unnameable" in the work of another author, further confounding real and imagined with a basis in what was surely a fantasy put forward in its day as truth.

10 Here Lovecraft makes it clear that monsters are not just scary "others" but are something best kept hidden. The idea of a monster as a "dirty little secret" was a recurring theme well before Lovecraft's time, and it persists today. It certainly has its roots in the sequestration of physically and mentally handicapped children that has been common practice throughout history.

11 A monster can sometimes be defined as an animal we haven't seen yet, and this description of the effects of the attack, which draws similarities to recognizable animals and gives the sense that people were searching for a rational explanation based on signs left behind, plays into that idea nicely.

er unlocked that attic door, but left the whole house as it was, dreaded and deserted. When noises came from it, they whispered and shivered; and hoped that the lock on that attic door was strong. Then they stopped hoping when the horror occurred at the parsonage, leaving not a soul alive or in one piece. With the years the legends take on a spectral character—I suppose the thing, if it was a living thing, must have died. The memory had lingered hideously—all the more hideous because it was so secret.[12]

During this narration my friend Manton had become very silent, and I saw that my words had impressed him. He did not laugh as I paused, but asked quite seriously about the boy who went mad in 1793, and who had presumably been the hero of my fiction. I told him why the boy had gone to that shunned, deserted house, and remarked that he ought to be interested, since he believed that windows retained latent images of those who had sat at them. The boy had gone to look at the windows of that horrible attic, because of tales of things seen behind them, and had come back screaming maniacally.

Manton remained thoughtful as I said this, but gradually reverted to his analytical mood. He granted for the sake of argument that some unnatural monster had really existed, but reminded me that even the most morbid perversion of nature need not be unnamable or scientifically indescribable.[13] I admired his clearness and persis-

---

12 Again, the threat of the monster is always more frightening than the monster itself, but even when Lovecraft recognizes this fact, it doesn't diminish the dread of the unknown.

13 Compare this to the movie *Alien,* in which we're first confronted by some kind of unknown animal, the so-called "face hugger," that the crew of the *Nostromo* approach as a medical problem. But as the situation gets out of hand and the thing reveals itself to be a vicious and single-minded predator, it feels more and more like a "monster" and less like an animal. Seeing a character like Manton try to bring human logic and scientific rationality to the problem makes it all the more frightening if or when a more visceral or unexplainable aspect of the creature is revealed. We humans tend to see the world around us as a series of problems to be solved—a monster that's "unsolvable" is truly terrifying.

tence, and added some further revelations I had collected among the old people. Those later spectral legends, I made plain, related to monstrous apparitions more frightful than anything organic could be; apparitions of gigantic bestial forms sometimes visible and sometimes only tangible, which floated about on moonless nights and haunted the old house, the crypt behind it, and the grave where a sapling had sprouted beside an illegible slab. Whether or not such apparitions had ever gored or smothered people to death, as told in uncorroborated traditions, they had produced a strong and consistent impression; and were yet darkly feared by very aged natives, though largely forgotten by the last two generations—perhaps dying for lack of being thought about. Moreover, so far as esthetic theory was involved, if the psychic emanations of human creatures be grotesque distortions, what coherent representation could express or portray so gibbous and infamous a nebulosity as the specter of a malign, chaotic perversion, itself a morbid blasphemy against nature?[14] Molded by the dead brain of a hybrid nightmare, would not such a vaporous terror constitute in all loathsome truth the exquisitely, the shriekingly unnamable?

The hour must now have grown very late. A singularly noiseless bat brushed by me, and I believe it touched Manton also, for although I could not see him I felt him raise his arm. Presently he spoke.

"But is that house with the attic window still standing and deserted?"

"Yes," I answered, "I have seen it."

"And did you find anything there—in the attic or anywhere else?"

"There were some bones up under the eaves. They may have been what that boy saw—if he was sensitive

---

14 Wow ... say that sentence ten times fast!

he wouldn't have needed anything in the window-glass to unhinge him. If they all came from the same object it must have been an hysterical, delirious monstrosity.[15] It would have been blasphemous to leave such bones in the world, so I went back with a sack and took them to the tomb behind the house. There was an opening where I could dump them in. Don't think I was a fool—you ought to have seen that skull. It had four-inch horns, but a face and jaw something like yours and mine."

At last I could feel a real shiver run through Manton,[16] who had moved very near. But his curiosity was undeterred.

"And what about the window panes?"

"They were all gone. One window had lost its entire frame, and in all the others there was not a trace of glass in the little diamond apertures. They were that kind— the old lattice windows that went out of use before 1700. I don't believe they've had any glass for a hundred years or more—maybe the boy broke 'em if he got that far; the legend doesn't say."

Manton was reflecting again.

"I'd like to see that house, Carter. Where is it? Glass or no glass, I must explore it a little. And the tomb where you put those bones, and the other grave without an inscription—the whole thing must be a bit terrible."

"You did see it—until it got dark."

My friend was more wrought upon than I had suspected, for at this touch of harmless theatricalism he started neurotically away from me and actually cried

---

15 Despite the horned skull, we're still hearing about this creature through the narrator's assumptions. And in this way—the idea that fiction is stranger than truth—the monster exists where monsters "really" exist: in the minds of the terrified.

16 Take note of this classic example of "show" vs. "tell." Lovecraft doesn't tell us, "That gave Manton the creeps." Instead he shows the physical effect on Manton and leaves us to interpret that it gave Manton the creeps based on the surrounding context.

out with a sort of gulping gasp which released a strain of previous repression. It was an odd cry, and all the more terrible because it was answered. For as it was still echoing, I heard a creaking sound through the pitchy blackness, and knew that a lattice window was opening in that accursed old house beside us. And because all the other frames were long since fallen, I knew that it was the grisly glassless frame of that demoniac attic window.[17]

Then came a noxious rush of noisome, frigid air[18] from that same dreaded direction, followed by a piercing shriek just beside me on that shocking rifted tomb of man and monster. In another instant I was knocked from my gruesome bench by the devilish threshing of some unseen entity of titanic size but undetermined nature; knocked sprawling on the root-clutched mold of that abhorrent graveyard, while from the tomb came such a stifled uproar of gasping and whirring that my fancy peopled the rayless gloom with Miltonic legions of the misshapen damned. There was a vortex of withering, ice-cold wind, and then the rattle of loose bricks and plaster; but I had mercifully fainted before I could learn what it meant.[19]

Manton, though smaller than I, is more resilient; for we opened our eyes at almost the same instant, despite his greater injuries. Our couches were side by side, and we knew in a few seconds that we were in St. Mary's Hos-

---

17 This calls up our discussion of invoking the five senses in the description of a monster. Lovecraft is describing the horrible *sound* it makes.

18 And next, a terrible smell. The word *noisome* was probably just as obsolete in Lovecraft's day as it is now, but basically it means "smelly." And because we know that the air both smells bad and feels cold, two of our senses have been activated in a single sentence.

19 It's interesting that Lovecraft still hasn't told us what this thing looks like, and that's surely intentional. People tend to be more reliant on sight than any other sense, and the idea of something you can hear, smell, and feel—but not see—is pretty scary.

pital. Attendants were grouped about in tense curiosity, eager to aid our memory by telling us how we came there, and we soon heard of the farmer who had found us at noon in a lonely field beyond Meadow Hill, a mile from the old burying ground, on a spot where an ancient slaughterhouse is reputed to have stood.[20] Manton had two malignant wounds in the chest, and some less severe cuts or gougings in the back. I was not so seriously hurt, but was covered with welts and contusions of the most bewildering character, including the print of a split hoof. It was plain that Manton knew more than I, but he told nothing to the puzzled and interested physicians till he had learned what our injuries were. Then he said we were the victims of a vicious bull—though the animal was a difficult thing to place and account for.

After the doctors and nurses had left, I whispered an awestruck question:

"Good God, Manton, but what was it? Those scars—was it like that?"

And I was too dazed to exult when he whispered back a thing I had half expected—

"No—it wasn't that way at all. It was everywhere—a gelatin—a slime yet it had shapes, a thousand shapes of horror beyond all memory. There were eyes—and a blemish. It was the pit—the maelstrom—the ultimate abomination. Carter, it was the unnamable!"[21]

If this is your first taste of H.P. Lovecraft, here's hoping it won't be your last. When I asked my friend Richard Baker what his favorite monster story or novel was, he answered, "'The Dunwich Horror.' I'm a big

---

20 And why *not* on the site of an ancient slaughterhouse?

21 Ah, finally, we find out what it looks like. But Manton's description is made all the more unsettling by both specific information—it had eyes—and Manton's desperate attempt to put it into words. Finally he refers back to the title, "The Unnamable."

Lovecraft fan, and that was the best monster story he wrote. Many of Lovecraft's stories lack immediacy; the threat is always subtle, implied, still developing, rarely seen in its entirety, or shown doing horrible things. In 'The Dunwich Horror,' Lovecraft shows the reader what a horror from alien dimensions can actually do when unleashed on a backward little New England town, and it's not pretty. The story also develops in a classic arc of origin, discovery, disaster, confrontation, and final revelation. Not many writers have used the formula to create such shocking and unearthly monsters as Wilbur Whateley or his unnamed brother."

Lovecraft was a master of the monster, indeed. Now let's all go out and work toward being masters of the monster ourselves.

A MONSTROUS STYLE GUIDE

Here are some craft tips and style suggestions to help you and your editor present monsters in a consistent and logical manner.

HE/SHE/IT

Is a monster a "he"? A "she"? Or is it an "it"? A good general rule of thumb is that a monster (or any animal) is referred to as "it" until its gender is both known and significant or when that monster gets a proper name.

For example, we know that Kong is a "he" not just because of his stalkeresque attraction to Anne Darrow, but because he has a name and is known to be a "he" by his worshipers.

Some sort of amorphous creature like Lovecraft's Shoggoths likely don't have any gender at all, so should always be referred to as "it."

Monsters that are transformed humans, like zombies, might be referred to in dialogue as "he" or "she" by individuals who once knew the human, but in general these beings soon become an "it." This gender-neutral pronoun has a tendency to keep things at a distance and implies that we're reluctant to, or unable to, assign this "thing" a gender. Once you start thinking of the Shoggoth as a girl, it starts to get a little less scary, a little less alien. And the reverse is true. When your hero's girlfriend dies and turns into a zombie and "she" turns into "it," the transformation is complete in the eyes of the hero: The girlfriend is gone, fully replaced by the monster.

CAPITALIZATION

A good rule of thumb when creating new things—monsters, animals, ranks and titles, and so on—is rather than create a new rule of grammar and usage to go with it, simply find the nearest real-world analog to that new thing and follow that rule.

For monsters, we'll want to fall back on the rules for animals. Though we've seen a few examples, especially from H.P. Lovecraft, where the names of the monsters were capitalized, I suggest you let that be another of his quirks.

So if you've created a monster called a "bloodstalker," and it's clear that there's more than one bloodstalker out there, it would be bloodstalker, lowercase *b*, the same way the *b* in *bear* would be lowercase if your characters were being hunted by a bear.

A possible exception would be if in some way that was a sort of brand name—appropriate maybe in science fiction but likely never in fantasy. So Dr. Morpheus has created the Bloodstalker, and you'd use the initial cap the same way you would for, say, a make of car: Dodge Caravan or Plymouth Destructinoid.

Of course, if the monster has a proper name, like my name is Phil, then you would follow that basic rule, i.e., Kong, Godzilla, etc.

LOVECRAFTISMS

H.P. Lovecraft contributed the article "Literary Composition" to the January 1920 United Amateur Press Association[1] in which he wrote:

> One superlatively important effect of wide reading is the enlargement of vocabulary which always accompanies it. The average student is gravely impeded by the narrow range of words from which he must choose, and he soon discovers that

---

1 See: www.brainpickings.org/index.php/2013/01/11/h-p-lovecraft-advice-on-writing/ and Writings in the United Amateur 1915–1922

in long compositions he cannot avoid monotony. In reading, the novice should note the varied mode of expression practiced by good authors, and should keep in his mind for future use the many appropriate synonymes he encounters. Never should an unfamiliar word be passed over without elucidation; for with a little conscientious research we may each day add to our conquests in the realm of philology, and become more and more ready for graceful independent expression.

To that end, here, courtesy of the website Cthulhu Chick,[2] are some of H.P. Lovecraft's favorite monstrous words, along with the text from the story in which the word is used.

ABNORMAL: "With Akeley's permission I lighted a small oil lamp, turned it low, and set it on a distant bookcase beside the ghostly bust of Milton; but afterward I was sorry I had done so, for it made my host's strained, immobile face and listless hands look damnably abnormal and corpselike." —"The Whisperer in Darkness"

ACCURSED: "The second voice, however, was the real crux of the thing— for this was the accursed buzzing which had no likeness to humanity despite the human words which it uttered in good English grammar and a scholarly accent." —"The Whisperer in Darkness"

AMORPHOUS: "I saw when I staggered to my feet that the amorphous flute-player had rolled out of sight, but that two of the beasts were patiently standing by." —"The Festival"

ANTEDILUVIAN: "Sir William, standing with his searchlight in the Roman ruin, translated aloud the most shocking ritual I have ever known; and told of the diet of the antediluvian cult which the priests of Cybele found and mingled with their own." —"The Rats in the Walls"

---

2 Lovecraft, H.P. *The Complete Works of H.P. Lovecraft*. Washington, DC: Squid Studios, 2011. E-book. See: cthulhuchick.com

BLASPHEMOUS: "As it was he thought only of the blasphemous monstrosity which confronted him, and which all too clearly had shared the nameless fate of young Thaddeus and the livestock." —"The Colour Out of Space"

CHARNEL: "The scene I cannot describe—I should faint if I tried it, for there is madness in a room full of classified charnel things, with blood and lesser human debris almost ankle-deep on the slimy floor, and with hideous reptilian abnormalities sprouting, bubbling, and baking over a winking bluish-green spectre of dim flame in a far corner of black shadows." —"Herbert West: Reanimator"

CYCLOPEAN: "From below no sound came, but only a distant, undefinable foetor; and it is not to be wondered at that the men preferred to stay on the edge and argue, rather than descend and beard the unknown Cyclopean horror in its lair." —"The Dunwich Horror"

DAEMONIAC: "Animal fury and orgiastic license here whipped themselves to daemoniac heights by howls and squawking ecstacies that tore and reverberated through those nighted woods like pestilential tempests from the gulfs of hell." —"The Call of Cthulhu"

EFFULGENCE: "And as I raised my glance it was without preparation that I saw glistening in the distance two demoniac reflections of my expiring lamp; two reflections glowing with a baneful and unmistakable effulgence, and provoking maddeningly nebulous memories." —"The Lurking Fear"

ELDRITCH: "The Thing cannot be described—there is no language for such abysms of shrieking and immemorial lunacy, such eldritch contradictions of all matter, force, and cosmic order." —"The Call of Cthulhu"

FOETID: "The thing that lay half-bent on its side in a foetid pool of greenish-yellow ichor and tarry stickiness was almost nine feet tall, and the dog had torn off all the clothing and some of the skin." —"The Dunwich Horror"

FUNGOID: "Three humans, six fungoid beings who can't navigate space corporeally, two beings from Neptune (God! if you could see the body this type has on its own planet!), and the rest entities from the central caverns of an especially interesting dark star beyond the galaxy." —"The Whisperer in Darkness"

GIBBERING: "And inside that rusted iron straitjacket lurked gibbering hideousness, perversion, and diabolism." —"The Unnamable"

INDESCRIBABLE: "On this now leaped and twisted a more indescribable horde of human abnormality than any but a Sime or an Angarola could paint." —"The Call of Cthulhu"

IRIDESCENT: "Two of the less irrelevantly moving things—a rather large congeries of iridescent, prolately spheroidal bubbles and a very much smaller polyhedron of unknown colours and rapidly shifting surface angles—seemed to take notice of him and follow him about or float ahead as he changed position among the titan prisms, labyrinths, cube-and-plane clusters and quasi-buildings; and all the while the vague shrieking and roaring waxed louder and louder, as if approaching some monstrous climax of utterly unendurable intensity." —"Dreams in the Witch-House"

LOATHSOME: "Hogs grew inordinately fat, then suddenly began to undergo loathsome changes which no one could explain." —"The Colour Out of Space"

LURKING: "For I, despite all you can say, and despite all I sometimes try to say to myself, know that loathsome outside influences must be lurking there in the half-unknown hills—and that, those influences have spies and emissaries in the world of men." —"The Whisperer in Darkness"

NAMELESS: "I had, it struck me, known all along that nameless horrors were gathering; that something profoundly and cosmically evil had gained a foot-hold under my roof from which only blood and tragedy could result." —"Medusa's Coil"

NOISOME: "Around the northern pole steamed a morass of noisome growths and miasmal vapours, hissing before the onslaught of the ever-mounting waves that curled and fretted from the shuddering deep." —"The Crawling Chaos"

SINGULAR: "Most of the time, the tread seemed to be that of a quadruped, walking with a singular lack of unison betwixt hind and fore feet, yet at brief and infrequent intervals I fancied that but two feet were engaged in the process of locomotion." —"The Beast in the Cave"

SPECTRAL: "But even so, the spectral horror was no less; for if these were living vermin why did not Norrys hear their disgusting commotion?" —"The Rats in the Walls"

SQUAMOUS: "The back was piebald with yellow and black, and dimly suggested the squamous covering of certain snakes." —"The Dunwich Horror"

TENEBROUS: "And through this revolting graveyard of the universe the muffled, maddening beating of drums, and thin, monotonous whine of blasphemous flutes from inconceivable, unlighted chambers beyond Time; the detestable pounding and piping whereunto dance slowly, awkwardly, and absurdly the gigantic, tenebrous ultimate gods— the blind, voiceless, mindless gargoyles whose soul is Nyarlathotep." —"Nyarlathotep"

TENTACLED: "A pulpy, tentacled head surmounted a grotesque and scaly body with rudimentary wings; but it was the general outline of the whole which made it most shockingly frightful." —"The Call of Cthulhu"

UNMENTIONABLE: "This almost made him lose his hold through faintness, but a moment later he was himself again; for his vanished friend Richard Pickman had once introduced him to a ghoul, and he knew well their canine faces and slumping forms and unmentionable idiosyncrasies." —"Pickman's Model"

UNNAMABLE: "If the plain signs of surviving elder horrors in what I disclose be not enough to keep others from meddling with the inner Antarctic—or at least from prying too deeply beneath the surface of that ultimate waste of forbidden secrets and inhuman, aeon-cursed desolation—the responsibility for unnamable and perhaps immeasurable evils will not be mine." —"At the Mountains of Madness"

UNUTTERABLE: "Perhaps I should not hope to convey in mere words the unutterable hideousness that can dwell in absolute silence and barren immensity." —"Dagon"

Use them with care lest the spectral host of the unnamable dark drag you to their loathsome hellscape! Or as Lovecraft himself wrote:

> But in enlarging the vocabulary, we must beware lest we misuse our new possessions. We must remember that there are fine distinctions betwixt apparently similar words, and that language must ever be selected with intelligent care.

APPENDIX B

SUGGESTED READING

The following are reading recommendations from a selection of the interviewees who appear in this book.

LYNN ABBEY, CO-CREATOR OF THE BEST-SELLING THIEVES' WORLD MILIEU: "Zero Mostel's *Book of Villains*. Sadly, it's long out of print, and although it allowed me to see monsters in a new way, it didn't reveal anything I didn't already know about them. In a more traditional, informative sense, I don't have a single favorite book about monsters because I've never had a single favorite source for monstrous information. In the beginning, I encountered monsters piecemeal in movies, comic books, fairy tales, and myths. The first book I recall reading that was at least partially about monsters was Edith Hamilton's *Mythology*. If I wanted a feast for the eyes, I'd open Christopher Dell's *Monsters: A Bestiary of Devils, Demons, Vampires, Werewolves, and Other Magical Creatures.*"

BRENDAN DENEEN, AUTHOR OF *THE NINTH CIRCLE*: "Easy. *Grendel* by John Gardner. By a mile. It humanizes one of the most famous monsters in literature and also explodes all kinds of myths, concepts, and theories while doing so."

MARTIN J. DOUGHERTY, AUTHOR OF *SHADOW OF THE STORM*: "*The Time of the Dark* by Barbara Hambly. The Dark are both alien and monsters, they personify a primal fear (of the dark!), and their actions make perfect sense from their point of view. They're also utterly inimical to humans not because they're 'evil' but because that's how they are. It's also a great story with characters that you'd care about, which is important because if you don't care who the monster is munching on, it's not really scary."

DAVID DRAKE, AUTHOR OF *HAMMER'S SLAMMERS* AND OTHER BOOKS: "*The Angry Planet* by John Keir Cross, which I read when I was ten or eleven. His Mars has two intelligent species, the Beautiful People and the Terrible Ones. The latter are utterly monstrous: giant, malevolent cabbages with tentacles. The climax … is just as horrifying to me now as it was in 1956."

SOURCES CITED

Novels

Excession by Iain M. Banks

Miss Peregrine's Home for Peculiar Children by Ransom Riggs

Ghost Story by Jim Butcher

Valentine Pontifex by Robert Silverberg

Prey by Michael Crichton

The Dragonriders of Pern by Anne McCaffrey

Blackstaff by Steven E. Schend

The Night Lands by William Hope Hodgson

A Princess of Mars by Edgar Rice Burroughs

Harry Potter and the Prisoner of Azkaban by J.K. Rowling

The White Dragon by Anne McCaffrey

Frankenstein; Or, The Modern Prometheus by Mary Wollstonecraft Shelley

Dune by Frank Herbert

Against a Dark Background by Iain M. Banks

The Coldest Girl in Coldtown by Holly Black

The Haunting of Dragon's Cliff by Philip Athans & Mel Odom

Dragonflight by Anne McCaffrey

Jurassic Park by Michael Crichton

A Wizard of Earthsea by Ursula K. Le Guin

Red Nails by Robert E. Howard

Cujo by Stephen King

The House on the Borderland by William Hope Hodgson

Short Stories

"The Little Green God of Agony" by Stephen King

"The Cold Step Beyond" by Ian R. MacLeod

"The Wendigo" by Algernon Blackwood

"The Double Shadow" by Clark Ashton Smith

"Leinigen Versus the Ants" by Carl Stephenson

"Pretty Monsters" by Kelly Link

"The Woman Who Fooled Death Five Times" by Eleanor Arnason

"The Damned Thing" by Ambrose Bierce

"The Variable Man" Philip K. Dick

Nonfiction

On Monsters and Marvels by Ambroise Paré

"The 'Uncanny'" by Sigmund Freud

The Hot Zone by Richard Preston

Killing Monsters: Why Children Need Fantasy, Super Heroes, and Make-Believe Violence by Gerard Jones

The Natural History of the Vampire by Anthony Masters

Etc.

Book of Pages by David Whiteland

Primeval Thule Campaign Setting (Sasquatch Game Studio LLC)

Advanced Dungeons & Dragons Dungeon Master's Guide by Gary Gygax

The Stories of H.P. Lovecraft

"The Unnamable"

"The Other Gods"

"Pickman's Model"

"The Whisperer in Darkness"
"The Shadow Out of Time"
"Dreams in the Witch-House"
"At the Mountains of Madness"
"Beyond the Wall of Sleep"
"Dagon"
"The Shadow Over Innsmouth"
"The Dunwich Horror"
"The Dream-Quest of Unknown Kadath"
"Herbert West: Reanimator"
Writings in the United Amateur 1915–1922

SELECTED INDEX